PRAISE FOR
THE ESSENTIAL DIVERSITY MINDSET

"With engaging storytelling and actionable practices to implement in your business, Soo Bong Peer's new book is the one that needed to be written for our society."

—Marshall Goldsmith, #1 *New York Times* bestselling author of *Triggers, Mojo,* and *What Got You Here Won't Get You There*

"There has never been a more important time than now for the valuable insights in *The Essential Diversity Mindset.* This book is a gift for anyone who works with people."

—Barbara Mitchell, coauthor of *The Big Book of HR* and *The Essential HR Handbook*

"*The Essential Diversity Mindset* delves into the psychology of diversity and inclusion as a transformative approach to human connection and the dismantling of systemic biases. This book resonated with my drive to increase equitable best practices in workplaces and communities, which spearheaded the launch of the National Diversity Council. I highly recommend this book that will change your perspective on race, ethnicity, and diversity beyond America's mental constructs."

—Dennis Kennedy, founder and chair of the National Diversity Council

"In *The Essential Diversity Mindset,* Soo Bong Peer brings her engaging and provocative voice to the global discussion on equity, inclusion and diversity. She wisely purports that an expanded approach—and new mindset—is needed to create organizations and communities where each person can thrive and where new heights of accomplishment are achieved. I highly recommend this book not only for evangelists of equity, diversity, and inclusion but also for anyone who wishes to increase their impact as a leader."

—Kristin Colber-Baker, global director of diversity, equity and inclusion, Mars, Inc.

"Soo Bong Peer eloquently weaves lifetime stories of her experiences from around the world to portray a path to bring people together in a rich fabric of diversity. This book should be of interest to leaders, managers, academics, or anyone else who wants to explore alternate ways to thrive in differences."

—Deepa Purushothaman, diversity, inclusion, and equity leader and former Deloitte partner

THE ESSENTIAL DIVERSITY MINDSET

HOW TO CULTIVATE A MORE INCLUSIVE CULTURE AND ENVIRONMENT

SOO BONG PEER

foreword by Clarence Page

This book is dedicated to my loved ones and the countless people I encountered from all walks of life who helped me to see and grow.

This edition first published in 2021 by Career Press,
an imprint of
Red Wheel/Weiser, LLC
With offices at:
65 Parker Street, Suite 7
Newburyport, MA 01950
www.careerpress.com
www.redwheelweiser.com

ISBN: 978-1-63265-189-1

Library of Congress Cataloging-in-Publication Data available upon request.

Cover design by Kathryn Sky-Peck
Cover illustration by iStock.com
Interior by Timm Bryson, em em design, LLC
Typeset in Warnock Pro

Printed in the United States of America
IBI
10 9 8 7 6 5 4 3 2 1

CONTENTS

FOREWORD

I am amused to think of how little I might seem to have in common with Soo Bong Peer.

I'm a black American journalist, born and raised in a midwestern factory town before I migrated to the big city. She was the daughter of a South Korean army general who became an ambassador to Mexico before she ended up in America. But we met through a classic American way: Our sons were high school buddies.

And we both share a love for this country's proverbial "melting pot," although I prefer such modern labels as the "salad bowl," the "gumbo," or the "mulligan stew." After all, the meat and vegetables in a stewpot don't totally melt together. They keep their identities, yet all lend flavor to the stew and receive flavor from it, too. It is that flavor that makes the stew special, like America.

Yet, our diversity is a paradox. We go back and forth as to how much it matters and whether it shouldn't. There was a great sense of relief embedded in the happy talk of a "post-racial society" after President Barack Obama's election. But no one says that now. One person's "post-racial" turned out to be someone else's "too racial."

New waves of headline-making racist, sexist, anti-Semitic, and otherwise xenophobic unrest signal how much more effort is needed to help Americans to live comfortably with our own diversity.

The most important stories in this larger challenge unfold not in the headlines but in the day-to-day lives of ordinary Americans. Great progress has been made to equalize opportunities and sensitize ourselves to our various tribal differences. Yet too many of us continue to harbor unresolved anger, fears, resentments, and suspicions.

In short, we need to talk. Unfortunately, our racial labels and other group identifiers, created to ease interracial dialogue, too often have served instead to pull us apart, sometimes exaggerating differences instead of bridging them.

To help us rebuild those bridges, Soo Bong Peer offers *The Essential Diversity Mindset,* a rich combination of personal stories, research data, and excellent advice to help us think and talk beyond the limits of labels to see, respect, and appreciate the individuals within.

If anyone knows about labels—or defying them—it is Soo Bong Peer. Born the daughter of a South Korean army general who became ambassador to Mexico, she became a writer, a consultant, an executive coach, a mother—and an American.

Yet, an early and defining theme in her book is her weariness with racial labels. It is not the use of such labels that troubles her as much as their overuse. When the labels become cages of confusion, confining our perceptions of others into boxes to be checked on a census form, she tells us, they actually impede our ability to appreciate others as individuals.

Her life journey takes us with her to different countries and social contexts, much as her life did, and examines what diversity means in different times and places. Her education into the salad bowl of race, ethnicity, and class—and responsibilities and obligations—becomes our journey, too.

She takes us from the process of indoctrination into various scripts to the special skill sets of "cross-cultural agility" and "pervasive diversity," the point at which we begin to gain maximum appreciation for life beyond the limits of our monolithic comfort zones.

"Let us be dissatisfied," Reverend Doctor Martin Luther King, Jr., preached in his last days, "until integration is not seen as a problem but as an opportunity to participate in the beauty of diversity."

In that spirit, I applaud this book. I often have compared race talk to sex talk: Everyone is interested in it, we like to think we're experts at it, yet we're reluctant to discuss it in mixed company or in front of the children.

Instead, we often try to keep the conversation within our own tribe, among people very much like us, which means a lot of dangerous myths and misunderstandings circulate among those of us who are too ignorant to know any better—and the bad news only gets worse.

Reading about Soo's life in this book may remind you, as it constantly reminded me, of your own experiences in America's great gumbo of diversity. Some of these stories are tragic. Others are hilarious, as absurd as our rules of racial etiquette can be in our society.

This book is as multifaceted as the challenges that race continues to pose in our society. In that sense it stands as a monument to a forward-looking motto that I heard a black civil rights leader tell a racially mixed audience: "We came here on different ships, but we're in the same boat now."

—*Clarence Page*

Clarence Page is a syndicated columnist for the *Chicago Tribune* and member of the newspaper's editorial board. He won the Pulitzer Prize for commentary in 1989.

INTRODUCTION

In America today, everyone has a label (white, black, Asian, Hispanic, gay, straight, transgendered, Muslim, Indian, etc.), racial labeling being the most prevalent. Through time, racial policies have inadvertently propagated racial stereotyping, associations, and separations. We have been conditioned to automatically see and place people into racial categories that simplify individuals into a single characteristic: erasing the human being behind the label.

This is the first book to argue that ubiquitous racial labeling is a key systemic bias that has unintentionally contributed to our nation's racial divide. As a natural progression of diversity policies, labeling people based on race, ethnicity, or skin color has become such an integral part of America's mental construct that we don't even think about or consider it to be a bias.

Labeling by itself is not a problem—how else would we have a shorthand for anything? I'm not suggesting we reduce labeling through our vernacular; that's not possible or practical. I'm suggesting we start shifting the stereotyping associations attached with each racial label to the point where labels become irrelevant. It's not our vernacular that is the issue; it's the subliminal connotations behind labels that create problems. Labels don't need to change; it's how we interpret these labels and the context in which they are used that must shift. When labels are viewed as qualifications or as an identity, we are no longer treating people on the same level. True diversity requires one to become color and label neutral—to see people of different colors, races, genders, aptitudes, backgrounds, and talents as equal beings within our shared humanity. Whether you are a part of the majority or living as a minority, the ability to connect beyond labels and to see past differences is the key barrier to successfully living in diversity.

In 1967, my family left Seoul for Mexico City so that my father could take his position as South Korea's ambassador to Mexico. I was fourteen years old and the daughter of one of the most respected and powerful South Korean military and political leaders. Without realizing it then, I was beginning my journey into the complex world of diversity, transitioning from the racially homogenous society of South Korea to the Western world that I knew nothing about.

Since my first trip away from my home fifty-three years ago, I have journeyed a far distance not only physically but emotionally navigating through foreign places and seemingly dissimilar mindsets, all the while frequently feeling like an outsider. Initially, I thought I was learning about the particularity of unique cultures and people. I didn't know it then, but what I was really absorbing was an understanding of humanity and the universality of being human. Whether interacting with locals in their own shops and towns in different parts of the world or working on partnerships or brand strategies in conference rooms with colleagues from Africa, Asia, Europe, Latin America, or North America, what I was soaking in was the binding force of our shared human essence and collaborative spirit. This force is what diversity is all about.

I discovered that regardless of where I was, no matter how different the people looked or spoke, people were still people. While there were external differences among us, there was nothing inherently different about the human condition, no matter one's culture, race, or socioeconomic class. I began to see beyond others' external differences and started seeing the human beings within, a perspective that is the foundation for building human connections and a world of pervasive diversity.

Inclusion and integration are fundamental cores that lie at the heart of diversity, be it in business, professional, government, or academic settings. However, in the name of inclusion and integration, our practices continue to divide, separate, and segregate people into racial labels and groupings. As we keep making superficial distinctions based on race, we keep enlarging boundaries that prevent people from coming together, diminishing a sense of belonging, and muddling fairness. Ironically, it seems that the diversity we are promoting is inherently segregated. We've forgotten about the melting pot and have moved on to individual ingredients that do not mix.

When we think about the word *diversity* in America today, it evokes sentiments of enforcements, legalities, and racial tensions. Instead, diversity should kindle feelings of connection, openness, and harmony among a wide spectrum of differences united by universal human similarities. The need to look at diversity in a different light is paramount—to see beyond ideals, rules, entitlements, and compliances.

Diversity and race relations have reached a boiling point that has become the central focus in America today. Race-related police shootings, white nationalist protests, violent riots, college demonstrations, killing of police officers, and the stifling of free speech are just some of the many symptoms of our divided country. It is alarming to witness the extent of racial divides spurred by the injustices and conflicts that are spreading through the fabric of our lives in America like a malignant lesion.

We should ask ourselves: Why is America's racial divide getting worse when there has been so much attention on promoting diversity? Why are we still living with racial divides, anger, and distrust after decades of diversity efforts? How can we better accept and live among all our differences in a society that is increasingly becoming more multiracial and multicultural?

Determining the best way to nurture inclusion is one of the most vexing issues facing every organization and our nation. How can we see diversity in a different light—beyond our programmed ideals, paradigms, entitlements, and compliances? When current policies and approaches do not produce the desired results, we owe it to ourselves to search for alternatives even in the face of potential disruptions, discomforts, and fears.

Diversity cannot be forced; it must be voluntary. When behaviors and mindsets are forced, we cannot expect genuine or sustainable change. The way I see diversity being promoted today has mostly been through righteousness, moral judgment, and negative reinforcement. We see terms such as *racist, bigot, sexist,* and *snowflake* being thrown around as commonplace, which only incites more anger and divide. If we were to raise a child this way, it wouldn't be a surprise to see either overt or silent anger and rebellion that would most likely yield undesirable consequences. We can anticipate a different outcome of rearing a child between a parent who judges, shames, and enforces their expected behaviors onto their child and a parent who guides their child toward positive results with empathy, open-mindedness, and understanding. This same logic applies to advancing diversity and inclusive cultures. We must foster, not force.

Diversity is a mindset, not a formula. Every person brings with them a unique history and background that shapes the way they see and interact with others. Unconsciously, from birth, we develop an attachment to the world that has been presented to us that creates the foundation for the way we perceive, behave, and react. Regardless of race, religion, or social class, we are programmed to see, judge, and make assumptions within seconds of meeting a new person. When cultures and individuals start to develop biases and prejudices, it's hard not to fall into that mindset. We must accept our flawed nature and sympathize with those who are unaware of their own prejudices. However, the more that people can broaden their mindsets beyond their current ideologies, beliefs, and biases, the better chance we have toward building a unified world.

The core challenge of diversity lies in reconciling our internal and external realities. While individual mindsets largely drive pervasive diversity, we cannot help but to be affected by the environments we inhabit. Culture, social climate, government policies, and systems are shifting the way individuals see their place in society. In order to change our mindsets and associations, we need a combination of personal and systemic change. Many may believe that formulas, programs, and training can solve our diversity challenges, but diversity is not quantifiable; it's intangible. The current analytical framework and mentality is the same that we employ to government policies such as health care, education, and tax reform, and yet we are still nowhere close to solving any of these issues. When we deal with individual feelings, it's unrealistic to assume we can solve our intangible diversity intricacies with a formula, an ideology, or rules.

Successful diversity is about comfortably connecting to people who are different from us, expanding what we are willing to be open to, and cultivating an inclusive culture in which people feel at ease with being themselves. Diversity does not just entail race and gender, it also includes diversity of perspectives, beliefs, and opinions. While we can stay true to our core beliefs, we must also be able to acknowledge difference of thought without passing harsh judgment or denouncement, no matter how contrary they may be to our own. I don't believe there is a simple, analytical, or all-encompassing solution to solving diversity. However, we must consider policies and programs that infuse human emotion, behavior, and psychology. We must nurture those elements that connect us, and reduce those that divide us, through leadership, individual growth, and system changes.

I am not black. I am not white. I am not Hispanic or Native American. I come from an Asian culture with a global perspective and see the racial divides that the United States is facing through a unique lens. In the forty-eight years in which I have lived in this country, I have never been more worried about where we are. Although my label may be along the lines of an Asian-American woman, this does not define me. Just like everyone else on this planet, I am far more than my skin color, gender, or label. I am a mother, a wife, a writer, a daughter, a sister, a friend, an executive coach, and a consultant.

As we navigate our unhealthy atmosphere with intensifying ruptures that are tearing our country apart, I hope this book will resonate with those who are concerned about the current social climate, whether they be on the left, the right, or somewhere in the middle. In this book I share my experiences, observations, and knowledge about human dynamics that underlie our divide and connection. *The Essential Diversity Mindset* will benefit anyone who is interested in expanding their awareness of self and the psychology that manifests racial tensions, diversity complications, and cross-cultural challenges.

Through my varying exposures and personal experience of negotiating diversity, I offer a different outlook that may be helpful as you journey within our constantly evolving world. I know how it feels to be different and I know what it's like to deal with differences. My hope is that my outlook and insight might inspire a pause for reflection, shift perspectives, and heighten awareness of the thoughts and emotions that run through you.

The most pivotal lesson I have learned throughout my journey is: I am who I think I am, not how I think others see me. We must first feel at home within our own skin before we can feel at home in the outside world. Regardless of how others viewed or treated me based on what they thought I represented—a daughter of a military general and foreign dignitary or an Asian immigrant minority woman—I was the same person. By subjecting my sense of self to the quick and superficial judgments of others, I was buying into a false reality. The truth is that we never know what others are thinking.

I hope to reach those who feel different or alienated and want to nourish self-empowerment; those who desire to expand their empathy and agility to connect; and those who want to deepen their capacity to lead others through compassion and open-mindedness. I believe that together we can find alternatives to shift mindsets and societal norms, nurture diversity through voluntary desire, and build an inclusive society that will allow us to unite through the common human essence.

—*Soo Bong Peer*

DIVERSITY AND DIVIDES

1

DIVERSITY IN CHANGING TIMES

Evolving the State of Mind

After sixty years, still etched into my memory is the image of a well-dressed forlorn-looking black boy of seven or eight years old, standing by himself. It remains like a vivid movie scene in my heart. I don't even know his name. I was seven years old, and this boy changed my perspective and sense of awareness in a single moment.

The year was 1959 in Busan, South Korea, a city still reeling in the aftermath of the Korean War. There were hardly any telecommunications other than the telephone and Korean radio and there was, of course, no television. Other than the postwar US military that was stationed within our country, South Korea was completely homogenous in race—as was China and Japan. As a child, my friends and siblings used to stop and stare in awe at the Americans when we ran into them. We would giggle and point at their silky, unfamiliar "yellow hair." Their blue eyes scared us; they were unlike anything we'd ever seen before.

Emerging from three years of bloody war that ended in 1953, South Korea was heavily dependent on US aid and military protection. Having an association with an American organization or citizen was viewed as an honor. Lucky for me, my family had easy access to the US military base, as my father was then the chief of staff of the South Korean army. Along with my family's access, my grandmother spearheaded the creation of a reciprocal relationship between my elementary school and the elementary school within the US military base. My grandmother wanted to provide venues where I was exposed early to the Western world so I could expand my boundaries and become worldly.

One day, my classmates and I got to visit the US military base and meet all the American children. In our group were about fifteen children between the ages of seven and nine. Only select students were chosen to participate for this occasion. Even though I was the youngest, thanks to my grandmother's special relationship with the school on the US military base, I was picked to be the leader of the group. You can imagine my excitement! That day, my classmates brought special gifts for the American children and dressed in special outfits: girls in traditional Korean dresses and boys in formal suits. When we arrived at the school, the American teachers welcomed us and introduced the American children to us. I had never seen so many Western people at once. We gave the students our gifts and then went out to play.

On the playground, something struck my eye—a boy standing all by himself. His eyes were downcast, shy, and seemed full of sadness. I still vividly remember feeling sad for him deep in my heart, not knowing why. I decided to approach him. As I walked toward him, I suddenly realized that his skin color was a much darker complexion than the other American children—he was the first black person I had ever met. I shyly stood before him and gave him a gift. Since we didn't speak each other's language, we could only smile and nod. Yet I immediately felt a connection with him. Our interaction lasted only a few minutes, but this moment deeply shifted my sense of awareness.

I grew up in a different time and place. As surprising as it may sound in today's world, all I knew about race up to this point was within the sphere of Asia. In today's America, children are exposed early on to a variety of ethnicities and races on television, on the internet, or in classrooms. We were not yet exposed to other races.

As children, our understanding of the world is shaped primarily by the environment we are brought up in. Generally, children accept the world they are presented because they know nothing else outside of their bubble. I didn't even realize this boy was black—he was just another American who happened to have darker skin.

That day, without realizing it, I dipped my toe into the world of racial diversity and racism. I recall sensing that somehow the boy's dark skin color might have something to do with him not being a part of the other children on the playground. Although I had seen segregation in South Korea in the form of socioeconomics, separation in the form of skin color was new to me. By stepping outside of my world, I was exposed to new people, ideas, and ways of thinking that changed my state of mind. I met the little black boy sixty years ago, but I see similar struggles in America today.

A Divided Nation

The population of the United States of America may be at its most polarized yet. According to a 2016 Gallup poll, 77 percent of Americans believe that the country is divided, a record high, up from the previous high of 69 percent in 2012.[1] In 2016, the four most important problems Americans identified were the economy, government, jobs, and race relations. This was the first time that race relations ranked that high.[2] Americans who say they personally worry a great deal about race relations have sharply risen in recent years: 17 percent in 2014, 28 percent in 2015, 35 percent in 2016, the highest in Gallup's eighteen-year trend at 42 percent in 2017, 37 percent in 2018, and 40 percent in 2019.[3] According to a 2019 Pew Research Center report, 58 percent of Americans' views of race relations were negative.[4]

Race has become one of the core conflicts facing America—a conflict that has been building since this country's founding. I do not believe race division is a singular issue; it is just the most pronounced in an intricate web of conflicts. Any healthy democracy should have diverging ideas and beliefs, but when diverging ideas create hostile attitudes and actions from opposing sides, we create divides, not bridges. When two sides are so deeply ingrained with their own ideologies, radical activists can become incapable of debate or hearing the other side.

The 2016 presidential election marked one of the ugliest periods in our nation's recent history. Never has there been an election during which the public was so vehemently split over their dislike of each candidate: businessman Donald Trump and former Secretary of State Hillary Clinton.

Before, during, and after the election, we witnessed the worst from the media, politicians, educators, husbands, wives, and family members all over the country. With the election so close to Thanksgiving, never have we heard so many reports of families refusing to speak to one another, close friends cutting ties, and relationships ending in heartbreak. As reported by Reuters, a woman in Bellingham, Washington, separated from her husband of twenty-two years after discovering that he voted for Trump. To this person and many others, being a Trump supporter was a dealbreaker. For many on the other side of the spectrum, being anti-Trump was also a dealbreaker. A Reuters/Ipsos poll of 6,426 people found that 16 percent of Americans had stopped talking to a family member or friend as a result of the election and 13 percent said they had ended a relationship.[5]

For both sides of the political spectrum, the 2016 presidential election was about much more than winning or losing—it would determine the direction of our country. Though the election encompassed many issues, such as the economy, immigration, health care, terrorism, national security, taxes, and identity politics, race relations may have been the most contentious and deeply emotional.

On one side, many believed Trump voters supported racism, sexism, and discrimination. On the other side, many believed Clinton voters supported identity politics and socialism. The candidates, political leaders, campaign managers, media, and public all fueled the unhealthy tension, fear, and hate to a toxic scale. If Trump won, many felt our country would take a giant step backward in regard to racism, discrimination, and intolerance. If Clinton won, many felt we'd be teetering on the edge of socialism and economic collapse. Two sides were fighting with life-and-death fear, and neither side would tolerate hearing the other.

When two sides are equally radical and unwilling to respect one another, whether we realize it or not, we are supporting division and spreading social harm. The election, and the beginning of Trump's presidency, is a somber reminder of how far we must travel to reach a place where we can have constructive conversations without attacking one another. For now, collaborative unity seems a far-removed possibility. This is a dangerous and alarming place to be.

I believe that the core catalyst for America's divide is rooted in race relations. More so than socioeconomics, more so than partisan government, race relations in the United States is the most heated and contentious subject facing our country. At the core of our divide is the tension between blacks and whites. It's impossible for me, or any person who is not black, to fully grasp what it means to be a black person in America. For centuries, being a black person in America meant that you had no place in America. We are the imprints of our history, and no other race in America has endured so much pain and discrimination. Times have changed, and although we are seeing shifts in mindsets and progress in diversity, the deep wounds from the past are still lingering and may never fully heal.

Our current diversity framework has rightfully been built to protect racial groups that have been underserved and discriminated against—a way to right the wrongs of the past and shift the social current toward increased equality and fairness. While the intentions have been altruistic, the results have been mixed. Through affirmative action, racial quota goals, and financial aid, we've attempted to reset the playing field and help those who need it most. Unfortunately, no system is perfect or can please everyone. Nevertheless, despite numerous diversity initiatives, we're experiencing heightened anger and divide that were unforeseen.

There is an enormous contradiction that needs to be addressed in regard to diversity progress. Over time, racial grouping has fostered a culture of pervasive labeling through identity categories, race boxes, and an overemphasis on racial differences. Racial labeling is a powerful divider that separates people into distinct classifications, as though the people in a certain race group are different from those in another. Aren't we all humans who share commonalities, and at the same time, possess uniqueness? Should our skin colors and physical differences be the determining factor to divide us? It may sound odd to blame racial labeling, but the problem is that by placing so much focus on race, race has become identity, not the person. The compounding issue is that racial labeling has become a shorthand for stereotyping unique individuals.

There is a difference between seeing the physical differences of others and defining a person with a label. If you can see with your eyes, then you will see the differences in others. To suggest we must become color blind is not physically possible. Yet we can become color neutral. By being color neutral, we still see the differences in others, but those distinctions become irrelevant. We see and interact with the person behind the label, not as a distinct race. The moment we start lumping everyone into groups is the moment of division. By separating ourselves into racial categories, we create an us versus them mentality.

It is frightening to witness the extent of America's racial, political, and cultural divide. We exist in a social climate that is so caught up with finger-pointing, resentment, and hostility that we are ruining the fabric of American life. Anger breeds only more anger. We are fueling destructive forces of agitation with stronger intensity by the day. It will be a dangerous place for everyone if rage and hostility become a societal norm.

As Martin Luther King, Jr., said so eloquently: "Returning hate for hate multiplies hate, adding deeper darkness to a night already devoid of stars. Darkness cannot drive out darkness; only light can do that. Hate cannot drive out hate, only love can do that."

What Is Diversity?

At its most basic definition, *diversity* means "variety": a variety of cultures, ideas, languages, races, and talents that cover every dimension of humanity. Beyond academic definitions, diversity is a mindset. Diversity is about how we view others and how we feel about ourselves in relation to others. We can choose to view a person as a unique individual or as a representative of his or her respective race. Unfortunately, our society seems stuck on the latter.

Diversity is not a public duty like recycling or following the law; it's about creating authentic human bonds, not fulfilling a quota or social obligation. Sadly, many treat diversity like they treat their taxes—as a bothersome but necessary duty. These people may not be racists, but when they are forced to meet quotas or act politically correct, they will do so not with their heart but out of a law-abiding obligation. When diversity is expressed with contrived attitudes and does not come from one's genuine heart, then that is not real diversity. People who receive contrived acts of kindness or diversity can tell the difference. Although people may do amazing things in the name of diversity, if they are doing it solely because they feel as though they are supposed to, then they are missing the entire point.

Diversity isn't about writing a check or putting in the time; it's about connecting with individuals on a daily basis with the mentality that people matter equally. The less you have to think about diversity, the more you connect with others. The truth is that we are far more similar than we are different, no matter how we may look or behave on the outside. When you interact with another person, regardless of where he or she may be from, you are first and foremost interacting with another human being who shares humanity.

Diversity cannot be forced; rather, it is a reflection of an individual's lens. Regulations and enforcements may drive certain outcomes, but they do not alter the mindset of individuals, the ultimate producer of sustainable change and diversity. The majority of all human conflict stems from individual interpretations that differ from one another. You never know what's going on inside another person's mind. How one interprets physical external differences such as color, size, shape, ethnicity, and gender is invisible to everyone else. It takes a certain capacity to see and honor human differences. Without it, we do not have diversity. If diversity is important to an individual, that individual will act on it and live an inclusive life regardless of affirmative action, equal opportunity mandates, or whatever social media activists say on Facebook or Twitter.

Sadly, the way we are using the term *diversity* has shifted away from its intended meaning and has mainly focused on gender and skin color; this is just scratching the surface. Identity politics has fueled and reinforced racial tensions because it uses race grouping as a shorthand to discuss everything. We are simplifying and dividing humans based on one dimension: race. This is a very binary way of looking at the world—black or white, good or evil, progressive or racist. How did racial divides become the front-and-center focus of diversity?

The Crossroads of Diversity in America

From my experience, the United States is the most accepting and least discriminating among all the countries in which I've lived and experienced, including those in Asia, Central America, and Europe. Many immigrants across diverse social strata who I have interacted with through the years have echoed the same sentiment. Of course, no system or place can be perfect. However, having seen discrimination in the racially homogenous society of South Korea and having experienced the country's oppressive military dictatorship that lasted almost thirty years, I appreciate the power and freedom of democracy in the United States every day.

My son, Michael, moved from Washington, DC, to Los Angeles. The first thing he criticized about California was not the weather; it was the lack of appreciation for the weather. If all you know is beautiful California weather and have never traveled outside of the state, then it would only be natural to take the weather for granted. In the same sense, I can imagine it might not be easy for those who have lived only within the United States and are accustomed to what it offers to see the full extent of our country's incredible acceptance and freedoms.

Years ago, my uncle and his family immigrated to America to give his son, who was born with limited intelligence and a dark mole that disfigured a large portion of his face, a place where he could be accepted. My uncle and aunt had tried every remedy—doctors, Chinese medicine, herbs, and whatever they heard could help their son, to no avail. You see, in South Korea, my cousin was regarded as substandard, bringing shame both for him and his family. In the 1980s, my uncle decided to emigrate from South Korea to America, where he knew his son would have a better life. In America, my cousin was given more opportunities and lived without the social stigma he would have experienced in South Korea. Before my uncle passed away, he told me on multiple occasions that moving to America had been one of the best decisions he'd ever made. There is no doubt in my mind that the United States embraces and accepts differences better than any other place I know.

When we live in a society as diverse as the United States, it is only natural that conflicting beliefs, biases, and prejudices will provoke disagreements, clashes, and separations. Every day, America is becoming more diverse and multiethnic. The more diverse a society, the greater the likelihood that tensions will exist. Although I believe America is still the most diverse and accepting country in the world, we are currently at a crossroads, facing an intense divide, with racial tensions that fuel hostility. Without significant mindset changes and measures that can influence public consciousness, the racial tensions and diversity challenges we're experiencing today are unlikely to abate.

The Experience of Changing America

In the aftermath of the Korean War, the United States provided extensive economic and military assistance to revitalize the war-torn country of South Korea. In 1954, as part of a joint military training program, several of the commanding generals, including my father, were invited to visit America. As a welcoming gesture, the American colonel who was assigned to escort the Korean generals decided to take them out for a lavish dinner. The colonel chose one of the most highly regarded steak houses in the Midwest. At the door, the Korean generals were denied entrance to the restaurant because they were deemed "colored." The colonel was mortified, feeling even more embarrassed than my father and his fellow generals. Years later in the 1980s, when I met that American colonel, who had since become one of my father's closest friends, he still felt ashamed over the incident that occurred so many years before.

In the early 1960s, in stark contrast to my father's experience of being discriminated against at the restaurant in 1954, the US government opened its arms to protect him. As the chief of staff of the South Korean army, he was dealing with heightened political instability and the agitation of many generals serving beneath him. Going against their wishes to overthrow the government, my father vehemently opposed the idea of a military dictatorship by means of a coup d'état. He believed in democracy and always said that killing only begat more killing. Regardless, the generals under my father conspired against him and successfully overthrew the government on May 16, 1961.

After the military coup, my father was placed under house arrest. Considering the influence and respect he had garnered in the past, he was viewed as a major threat to the fledging military power. I was only eight years old and did not understand why my father was home all of a sudden. Nonetheless, I was thrilled to be able to see him all the time. Although there was a sense of unease, I was overwhelmed with joy because I was finally able to play and spend time with my father, an experience that was rare for me. Some of my most cherished memories of him come from this tumultuous period that I will carry in my heart forever.

During the middle of the night, a month into my father's house arrest, I was awoken by a commotion. I walked out of my bedroom to see my father hugging my crying mother goodbye. I felt as if I was in a dream, I was so confused. My father gave me a quick hug and rushed out the door. I later learned that he was being secretly escorted by US military personnel to the US base, and flown to Washington, DC. The US government provided my father with political protection from potential assassination attempts. We remained safe in Seoul without my father.

My mother, my younger siblings, and I did not see my father again for four years while he was being protected in the United States. Until the day my father passed away, America held a very special place in his heart. Because of his respect and trust in America, he brought all four of his children to the United States for education in the 1970s and 1980s.

Times change, and we cannot dwell in the past. The America that discriminated against my father and other colored people in the 1950s and 1960s was changing. As a leader of South Korea, a homogenous society in which accepting differences may have presented a much harder road to attain, my father truly respected and appreciated America's resolve to implement changes that would mitigate future discriminations. My mother, siblings, and I have always been grateful to the United States for protecting my father, and we have carried his outlook as well.

Stains of Atrocities

Since the dawn of man, history is full of inequities, a reflection of the dark side of being human. Slavery can be traced back to ancient Egypt, China, Greece, and Rome, long before the United States. We've seen genocide after genocide from Adolf Hitler to Mao Zedong, and still today in Syria. In the end, civilizations move forward, rebuild over past devastations, and slowly heal broken spirits. For the victimized, it's natural to have feelings of rage, injustice, and the urge to retaliate. While we must not condone previous inequities, we cannot move forward by continuously condemning the past or by living in perpetual guilt.

A few years ago, I had a very heated conversation with my close friend Jodie. Throughout her life, she felt the burden of being discriminated against for being an African-American. As we were having dinner one night, the topic of slave reparations came up. Jodie said an argument could be made for the justification of reparations. I shared my opinion: we cannot let the past drive the future because both people and times have changed. Living with the anger of the stains of past atrocities only enlarges a sense of victimization and guilt from both sides. This emotional dynamic only intensifies resentment and hostility. Also, it's not possible to put a fair price point on the misery of your ancestors. I told her that we must move forward, and that no monetary value could erase the crimes of the past. People alive today do not have the same mindset toward slavery as people did two hundred years ago. If anything, most Americans feel slavery was one of the darkest periods in our nation's history. The only way to be liberated from the past, I said, is by moving forward, not backward.

Jodie told me how disappointed and hurt she was in my stance. Even though she's one of my closest friends, I could feel a rift growing between us. In her view, feeling discriminated against her whole life, she felt I didn't understand her and didn't support her. Her reaction made me very sad because she couldn't accept my belief on face value; rather, she was interpreting my opinion as a betrayal against her race. When people jump to such a rash conclusion, how can we possibly have constructive dialogues? I had spoken with no intention of expressing bigotry or prejudice and resented her for misinterpreting and misunderstanding what I had said.

I shared with Jodie my experiences about how my feelings about myself influenced whether I felt discriminated or not. What I learned was that how I felt about myself drove how I saw and interpreted others' attitudes. When I used to feel less about myself for being an Asian immigrant, others' body language and actions reflected my mental state. Gradually, as I built a stronger self-image and felt comfortable about who I was in America, others' attitudes reflected my sense of self. Of course, there will always be people who will be prejudiced against race, ethnicity, gender, or any other differences. I can't change them. The only party in the equation I have control over is myself. Admittedly, I was disheartened at first with Jodie's reaction to our conversation. I didn't feel she was open to hearing me.

Initially, Jodie felt I was lecturing her and said she was different from me. In her mind, Asians were less discriminated against than African-Americans and therefore I could not understand the plight of black people in America. I told her that I felt touched by how honest she was, even though what she felt might not be how I saw it. Through additional dialogues, we have deepened our friendship, understanding, and support for each other.

Jodie helped me to appreciate the depth of her struggles and resentment. I helped Jodie to express and reflect on her difficult and deeply personal feelings. What I wanted most was for Jodie to feel empowered by her own strength and worth as an individual, not to live out the stereotype of her label as a black woman in America. I believe living with a sense of victimization disempowers us.

Feeling discriminated against is something that spans cultures, races, socioeconomics, and social statuses. Prejudices and discriminations lie at the heart of diversity challenges. The example of my dialogues with Jodie portrays the fertile ground in which even close friends can feel discriminated against. It also demonstrates how easily we can be thrown into confusion and self-doubt for not knowing the best way to broach sensitive topics and fearing we may be seen as a biased or prejudiced person.

Fortunately, I had a close relationship with Jodie in which we could talk things out. However, if we didn't have open communication, I could have become more careful with Jodie the next time we got together, and not shared how I felt. That would have created a relationship where both of us were guarded and separate—far from a connecting place. It's difficult to erase the stains of past atrocities. They plant deep roots of generational anger that become entangled in a messy web of diversity challenges, despite the progress people have made.

Where We Are in America

America is a leader in promoting equality and human rights. Arising from outright discrimination and blatant social injustice, the civil rights movement marked the beginning of the diversity initiative in the United States. Since then, tremendous progress has been made throughout the past sixty years. People's mindsets have changed too. For example, interracial marriage was illegal in many states until the Supreme Court declared all laws prohibiting interracial marriage unconstitutional in 1967. Approval of interracial marriages, in particular between blacks and whites, has greatly shifted over the past fifty-five years. In 1958, the approval rate was 4 percent; in 2013, it was 87 percent.[6]

Today, America is still deeply divided by racial tensions. Could we be at a crossroad where well-intended diversity measures may have evolved to the point at which ideology may be trumping merit?

It appears that we've become so hypersensitive about policing diversity that we've forgotten to actually embrace it. I don't believe we can build open connections, genuine respect, or true human dignity on forced actions spurred by ideology, obligation, or guilt. What I just said may be considered racist by some, and to me, that is exactly a problem. I am not suggesting we strip away opportunities to racial minorities; I am talking about equality beyond race and gender. We've become so paralyzed by the fear of being viewed as racist that we have become blind to the repercussions of entrenched identity politics.

Regardless of race, color, gender, or socioeconomic status, I truly believe that most Americans care deeply about diversity. We are living in the 21st century with evolved mindsets. Yet we are facing immense challenges ahead with heightened racial divides and a social climate of anger. Any measures that were created in the past that no longer produce desired outcomes must be reassessed within the changing context of the present.

Essential Takeaways

- Times, mindsets, and demographics are changing, yet our nation's racial divide is getting worse despite years of effort promoting diversity. While the makeup of the United States is becoming ever more multiracial and multicultural, racial labeling and identity politics are keeping people divided. It seems apparent that we must redefine the meaning of diversity and evolve the ways we currently think about race, ethnicity, and progressiveness.
- Diversity can't be forced. True inclusiveness stems from voluntary acceptance. Our thoughts, feelings, and behaviors shape the diversity climate. We can never change the painful past; however, we can shift our perspectives and actions, and contribute in advancing a safer and more connecting place in life and at work.
- Our differences are what make us unique. Having a comfortable sense of self as a unique individual empowers us. Is it fair to define an individual based on external elements such as skin color and race, and thus erase the person inside? Take a moment and reflect on how prevalently our society predominately describes people: as a race or as an individual? What alternate approaches could nurture the quality of our interacting space that thrives in unity with differences?

2

BIASES AND PREJUDICES

Inherent in Being Human

No one is born a bigot or a racist. Every baby comes into this world with light and joy. Biases and prejudices are learned, not genetic. Every parent carries with them their own idiosyncrasies that shape their children. Preferences, ideologies, beliefs, humanity, and wisdom are just some of the characteristics we pass on to our children. Biases and prejudices are no different than other inherited scripts.

Today, if a person has a bias or a prejudice that is perceived to be racist or bigoted, there seems to be no empathy from those who are doing the condemning. Regardless of race or culture, we need to approach all people with the same humanity and compassion as we would our own selves. If you want someone else to listen to you, then you have to be willing to meet that person halfway and listen equally. Once you start to understand how that person became who they are, the possibilities for a dialogue expand. Most of the time, people are unaware of their own deep-seated biases or prejudices, because they are so deeply embedded into the fabric of who they are. If we want people to change their outlooks, biases, or prejudices, we must first understand how these attachments came to be and how we can move past them.

Many people have empathy, but when it comes to race and identity politics, some people have zero tolerance for anyone who they consider their enemies. You don't treat alcoholics or addicts with disrespect or condemnation. For all you know, their addiction is the manifestation of the unfortunate scripts they inherited. The same can be said for a racist, yet racists are not deemed worthy of healing or redeeming. Instead, we condemn them by screaming just as loud from the other side. We will not connect this way.

Rigid Attachment

When my husband, Steve, and I had our first child, Sophia, we had to work through the widely divergent child-rearing philosophies we brought from the homes in which we grew up. Our beliefs and values had become deeply ingrained, but they came from extreme opposite worlds and cultures.

Steve, a Caucasian American, grew up with parents who had German and Welsh heritage. Our parents raised us differently. My husband wasn't raised with the same kind of cuddling or attention I received as a toddler. His parents were afraid that their children would not become self-sufficient if they pampered them early on. They focused on instilling in him a strong sense of independence. In stark contrast, I was cuddled and held all the time, and was raised with the belief that parents should go out of their way to express their love and make the necessary sacrifices for their children. There is no right or wrong way to raise a child, but it quickly became apparent that our clashing approaches did not mesh.

The first area in which I noticed conflict was when we had to decide where our infant daughter would sleep. When I was growing up in South Korea, it was common for young children to sleep in the same room with their parents until they were around five years old. At that time, traditional Western beds with legs, frame, and a mattress were not part of the culture. Instead, Koreans used a thick individual bottom and top quilt that were usually stored in a closet during the day. At night, they were placed on the floor of the room. Each room had underfloor heat, called "ondol," a Korean traditional architecture design that transfers heat to the underside of the thick masonry floor. It was also traditional in Korean culture for the entire family to sleep in the same room. The sleeping order was my father closest to the door, my mother, the youngest child, and each child after that all the way to oldest. I can still feel that toasty and cozy feeling of my entire family sleeping together in the same room.

As soon as Sophia was born, Steve wanted her to sleep in a crib in her own room. That was the way he and his siblings were raised, and that's how my husband wanted his children to be raised. I felt this method was a cold mistake. It didn't take long before Steve acquiesced to my pleading and let our three-month-old daughter sleep with us in our bed.

Months later, during a phone call with his parents, Steve mentioned that our daughter was sleeping in the same bed as us. His parents were shocked and told him that if we kept this up, our daughter would never be able to take care of herself. They went as far as to say she would never get into college, never get a job, and that she would be dependent on us for the rest of her life. My husband's parents persuaded Steve to put our daughter back into her crib, and while I argued and struggled over this issue for several days, I ultimately gave in.

The first evening Sophia slept alone in her own room, she wouldn't stop crying. My instinct was to run to her, but I knew Steve would be angry if I did. After twenty minutes, I couldn't take it anymore. I got up and brought her into bed with us. Her top was soaked from her tears. I put her wet face next to my husband. Sophia rubbed her nose and face against his neck, sighed happily, and fell asleep. It brought Steve to tears, and he never forced her to sleep in a different room again. Until that night, my husband had never allowed himself to question his parents' values. This was a defining moment for him as he started to question the validity of their inflexible doctrines. From that night on, we moved my daughter's crib next to our bed until she turned three. At that time, we moved into a new home and she was so delighted with her new room that she decided on her own to sleep there alone.

Without being aware, Steve doggedly followed his parents' teachings that had shaped his beliefs, attitudes, and actions. Without questioning, we can act like robots, defending and adhering to our ingrained narratives that form our mindsets and attitudes. Despite Steve's attachment to the doctrines that were drilled into him, there was no bearing on the consequential outcomes. Sophia went to a good college, has a good job, and is very much independent.

Unconscious Adoption and Endorsement

Growing up in a prominent and powerful family in the 1950s and early 1960s in South Korea, I was accustomed to living with maids who served my family. The country was very poor when the Korean War ended in 1953. Our maids, many of them young girls no older than twelve, came from small, poor villages. Our young maids often would cry, missing their mothers and families. All of them were malnourished and had no previous education. After a few months of living with us, they would always gain weight. Although they may have been much healthier living with us, nothing could fill the void of missing their family and loved ones left behind.

In my young eyes, I saw no difference between these maids and myself. We were from the same country and of the same race. As a young child, I didn't know anything about their unfortunate circumstances, nor did I have any concept of the difference between poverty and wealth. For a long time, I carried a deep sense of guilt because of the advantages life had given me. Why was I being pampered while they worked all day? Why weren't they able to go to school like me?

Whenever I would ask my family these kinds of questions, I was told that they were lucky to be working for us because otherwise, they would have starved to death. Additionally, if a maid worked hard for a long enough time, it was custom for the family she worked for to pay for her wedding or give her money as a retirement gift. This was a major incentive for many maids and their families. By having a paid wedding, their chance for a good husband and better future increased dramatically. The rationale that our maids were lucky just to be with us became a part of my psyche.

I will never forget Hiya, one of the young maids who served my family and became my lifelong surrogate sister. Hiya came to our home in 1961 when she was twelve years old, only three years older than I. The two of us became close and shared many private moments together. Hiya told me about her life before she came to work for us. She lived in a small village in a two-room thatched-roof house with limited heat and no electricity. She was the second oldest of five children in her family—four girls and a boy.

Her older sister died at five years old from pneumonia due to the cold conditions and lack of resources. I remember how vividly she recalled sleeping through the freezing night, shivering under a quilt. For days, Hiya and her family would stretch out the few grains of rice they had in order to make a watered-down porridge that would barely feed everyone. Hiya had already become accustomed to going to bed with hunger pains. Sadly, Hiya's parents had to make a painful decision. They realized that the best chance Hiya had in life was to be sent away to a wealthy family so that she could work and survive on her own. For many months after Hiya came to our home, she cried, missing her loving family and grieving over her misfortune.

Slowly, the two of us developed what I felt was an inseparable bond, not one of obligation but of love. To me, there was no difference between us; the only difference I recognized was the hand we were each dealt with at birth. Whereas I felt we shared a loving bond, Hiya harbored secret resentment. I had everything while she had nothing: no family, no money, no education, no opportunities. How could she not feel anger toward me when my lifestyle constantly reminded her of what she did not have? I started to feel guilty for what was given to me, even though I had no control over the family I was born into. As much as I tried to sympathize with Hiya's feelings, her resentment radiated toward me like a dark undercurrent beneath the surface. My sense of her dislike for me made me guarded and acted as the barrier that prevented us from fully connecting.

On several occasions, I suggested to my grandmother that our maids go to school with me. Sternly, she scolded me for thinking that I was similar to our maids. She didn't want me to think that I was anything like those girls, which was very hard for me to understand at first. Once again, I was reminded that our maids were lucky enough to simply be working for us. Gradually, my grandmother's message became part of my unconscious beliefs that I belonged to a separate class from them.

Many years later, in the early 1980s, when I began an entry-level sales job at a technology company in the southern United States, I invited my sales team's assistant to lunch. As we were chatting and exchanging our backgrounds, she made an odd comment about how I got hired: "Well, I'm sure they would rather hire you than a black."

It took a few moments for me to digest what she had just said. Then, a lightbulb went off in my head and I thought, "Wow . . . discrimination goes on in every culture and every race." What struck me was how casually she said this to my face, without a second thought. I was completely taken aback, and for the first time understood the depth of black discrimination. What threw me off was that she said this with a smile and charm that was so innocuous. Then I slowly understood: The assistant's deep-seated bias was identical to my own in regard to our young maids. We both carried deeply ingrained scripts that became part of the fabric of who we were.

Let's look at these two different stories:

1. **My belief:** "Our family's maids are lucky to be working for us. They don't belong in my class."
2. **Assistant's belief:** "The company would rather hire you (an Asian) than a black."

Without blinking an eye, we both believed an entire race or class of people were inherently inferior to us. The assistant and I were both blind, unconsciously carrying deeply ingrained messages that had become part of our belief systems.

Once an idea, concept, or value enters one's belief system, it becomes second nature and long-lasting. The destructive nature of bias and prejudice is that we don't stop to question ourselves. I feel there is a general notion that if someone has a bias or prejudice, that person is deemed to be uneducated, flawed, and shameful. On the contrary, the assistant was a well-educated, friendly, and extremely helpful person. We can't blame her or me for not being able to remove our deep-seated beliefs overnight, especially those one is unaware of. It's like a treatable tumor. If detected early, we could reverse the course. If left undetected, the tumor will keep growing and spread its malignancy throughout the body.

My relationship with Hiya was complicated yet timeless. There was no question about our love for each other or about our separateness—one being served, the other serving. Hiya worked for my family for more than twenty years, serving us in South Korea, Mexico City, London, and Tokyo, until she eventually married in 1985.

Despite her sad circumstances and resentment toward my privileged life, Hiya was always there for me. My issues were nothing compared to hers, but Hiya was one of the very few people in my life who I could talk to about anything. In hindsight, I feel like a spoiled brat, dishing out all my personal problems to a young woman who had far worse problems. Nonetheless, she always listened and never showed impatience. Every moment we were together, she gave me her full heart and attention. I am still moved by and grateful for her loving capacity and the tenderness she showed me.

Unfortunately, Hiya passed away when she was only fifty years old. To this day, I miss her terribly. Growing up and as an adult, I felt closer to Hiya than to any member of my family. She may not have had a high level of education, but she possessed an inherent wisdom and generosity of heart along with her forgiveness, greater than most people I have encountered.

Hiya helped me broaden my sphere of awareness and deepen my understanding of humanity, a gift I will always treasure. Due to changing times and prosperity in

South Korea, there are no longer young girls working as maids. If Hiya had been born a little later, she would likely have had the opportunity for a different life.

Waking Up

As children, we accept the world that is presented to us, until we wake up. As I look back now, I wonder how I could have thought that working as a maid at the age of twelve could be considered lucky. Or how my sales team assistant could have thought black people were less qualified than Asian people because of their skin color.

I recall the moment I first awoke from my preconceived bias. Years ago, I was chatting with my husband (then my boyfriend) about my upbringing, and we got to the topic of my family's young maids, including Hiya. When Steve found out how young our maids were and the situation they were forced into, he was shocked, and needed a moment before he could speak. Steve told me point blank that he believed my family had committed a terrible and unethical act of child labor. I was flabbergasted! Not only was I clueless as to what had upset him so much, I couldn't believe he thought my family would do such a terrible thing.

From my perspective (which was the same as my culture's), by letting poor young maids work for us, we were saving them. From his perspective, we were taking advantage of a terrible situation. Looking back at both of our perspectives in that moment, I am fascinated by where his thoughts immediately went. Steve was coming from his American beliefs and values, not taking into consideration the circumstances of Korean society at that time. On the flip side, I was coming from my own values and was offended that he didn't even give me a chance to explain my side.

Upon reflection, I can see how deep my unconsciousness was. I was blind to a different perspective. In an unfortunate twist of fate, Hiya and I were caught in the poverty of our country, the necessity for survival, and our class mindset. Although my husband's viewpoint altered my way of thinking, he needed to broaden his as well. Even if my husband may not agree, he was able to see where I was coming from. No one is right or wrong, and we both benefited from broadening our perspectives and worldviews. Across the world, we assess, judge, and denounce others based on our own beliefs and values, often without stepping foot into another's sphere. It is easy to impose our own beliefs onto others from the surface, without knowing the depths of the water.

Rarely is anything as clear-cut as we think it is. For us to assess the past retroactively, by using today's framework to judge another time and place, is a gross simplification of human complexity. In the context of changing times with varying circumstances and histories, we may have to look at past events in a different light. We ought to do this without condoning or condemning, but by using an expanded sense of empathy to reduce anger and resentment.

The Impact of Fear

Fear is a primal emotion that we can trace back to the dawn of man. When we were hunter-gatherers, fear protected us and kept us alive. Regardless of age, no one is immune to fear and no one is above it. Consider what fear could do to a child. It cements our learned biases and doctrines in our mind at an early age, and builds a long-lasting lens through which we see ourselves and others. Through fear, we construct prejudices and separation that crush our early desire to belong and embrace. We witness the world through the repeated history of a fear-based mentality that has plagued humanity forever.

Shortly after Japan's attack on Pearl Harbor, President Franklin D. Roosevelt ordered that all Japanese-Americans living on the Pacific Coast of the United States be sent to internment camps. Roughly 120,000 Japanese-Americans, including children born in the United States, were forced to relocate from their homes into the camps from 1942 to 1946. Sixty-two percent of the Japanese interments were US citizens. The rest were first-generation immigrants born in Japan who were ineligible for US citizenship at the time.

Whether it rises up in an individual or an entire nation, fear impacts every one of us. While our actions may be considered wrong in hindsight, under the attack of fear, we can be pushed to irrational thinking and actions. I am not suggesting that President Franklin D. Roosevelt's decision was solely based on fear. While the president may have been doing what he thought was best to protect the country, the extreme nature of the order suggests to me that there was a component of fear as well. Fear creates biases, which can skew mindsets and actions.

At the time of this writing, the United States is experiencing a similar fear-based biased reaction against Muslims, born out of the threat of ISIS. Like the Japanese internment camps in the 1940s where innocent

Japanese-Americans were unfairly punished for the actions of Imperial Japan, we are racially profiling Muslims because of the extreme actions of radical Islamic terrorists. Are all Muslims and ISIS connected? Were all US Japanese-Americans responsible for Pearl Harbor?

History is repeating itself, and the fear instigated by ISIS and radical Islamic terrorism has created a blanket fear against Muslims. There are more than three million Muslims living in the United States today. Surely, it would be unrealistic to think all these Muslims should be regarded with suspicion. Irrational fear blinds us, which leads to potentially unjustifiable skewed perceptions and attitudes. While fear-based behaviors are often irrational and regrettable, we have to understand we are all subject to the same human psychology.

Fighting fear by inciting fear is not the answer. There is a reason why some of the most infamous figures in history used fear tactics to propel themselves into positions of great power. We must recognize the role fear plays in our psyche and how fear can drive our actions. By acknowledging the nature of fear, without condoning it, we can increase our understanding of those whose actions were blinded by fear. We cannot escape fear, for it is part of our nature. However, actions and manipulations that fuel fear in the name of fighting fear are irresponsible and hypocritical, regardless of whether they come from the news, our leaders, or our parents.

A Victim of My Own Bias

When I came to America for college in 1971, I carried with me a bias against Korean immigrants living in the

United States. While this may sound absurd, my bias stemmed from class mentality. At the time, Koreans who immigrated to the United States were considered failures because they couldn't succeed in their own country. They were looked down upon for moving to another country.

Upper-class families and individuals didn't want to be associated with immigrants. In fact, in 1986, a close Korean friend who was an executive for a US corporation declined an opportunity to obtain a green card. He was concerned that having a green card would reduce his class standing in Korea and affect his children's potential marriages into the Korean upper class. As a student studying in America, I refused to see myself as an immigrant, rather as a visitor studying abroad for a short period. I never fathomed living in America as a full-time immigrant, for that would have made me feel ashamed.

Even though I was only studying abroad, my parents were deeply worried that I would be discriminated against by Americans as just another immigrant. They believed that if I was perceived as a student from an upper-class family, my chance of being discriminated against would go down significantly. They did everything possible to make sure the distinction was made clear. They ensured I had the best clothing, the best car, and spared no expense. They encouraged me not to mingle with Korean immigrants who did not belong to my class; other wealthy Koreans were fine in their book. This convoluted universal mindset affects all races and all classes.

During my studies, I made sure to explain to every American I encountered that I was just studying abroad and that my family had never immigrated. The truth is that I am no different from any other Korean living in America. Whether an immigrant, a student, a visitor, upper-class, or lower-class, there is no difference between us. My class mindset had created an illusion that I was a special case, exempt and different from all other Korean immigrants who had left their country.

The Americans I met never comprehended the inner chaos and shame I was experiencing. Most of the people I met probably found it strange that I was constantly explaining myself as a non-immigrant. I knew many other Koreans who were trapped in this same drama of bigotry and have met many others from all different countries in the world who felt similarly. Even after I became a naturalized Asian-American, I still carried with me the attitude that I was not an immigrant. I was only deceiving myself through the depth of my own bias.

Upon reflection, I realize that I was alienating myself from myself, living disconnected as a foreigner within. I was the victim of my own bias. Think about how confusing this message must have been to my psyche: I am a Korean, but I cannot truly be Korean in America because it is shameful. How could I possibly connect with others if I wasn't allowed to be who I was? I assumed others saw me the same way I viewed Korean immigrants living in America, which was to say, not in a good light.

When my husband and I decided to get married, it became clear that I would stay in America permanently. I had to accept the fact that I was going to become a Korean immigrant, not a temporary visitor. For a long time, I felt an enveloping shame over my tangled-up sense of self, fighting a complicated emotional battle between past and present mindsets. Regardless of logic and reason, my emotional attachment to what I grew up learning was still a part of me for a long time.

A common misconception about biases is that they can hurt only those being discriminated against. In reality, the person who carries negative biases and prejudices is also harming themselves in addition to others. Believe it or not, every once in a while, I still experience a sense of unease about being a Korean immigrant, despite the fact that emigrated Koreans are now well received and respected in my home country.

To be liberated from our old biases requires a retraining of the brain. The biases I grew up with used to frequently throw emotional mud at me; now this happens very seldom. I came to realize my mental attitude, which channeled my biases toward Korean immigrants, was the damaging inner voice that became an inner judge against me. In short, bias is the enemy that strikes ourselves as well as others. As I became free of my own biases, I fully embraced my identity as a Korean immigrant and created a closer connection to myself, which allowed me to connect with others. I am no longer a victim of my own prejudices and the narrowly defined life I lived. Accepting oneself is the only way we can truly build bridges with others.

Real or Perceived Discrimination

There are few things more painful than experiencing discrimination firsthand. The scarring impacts of prejudice can have lifelong ramifications, permanently shifting one's lens and outlook on humanity. Once a person loses faith in humanity, it's hard to find it again. Often victims of extreme prejudice can come off as hostile or overly guarded.

For example, imagine a Latino boy walking down the street. He has been followed by a white bully who hits him over the head with a baseball bat. From that day forward, this Latino boy will most likely never forget that moment. It's not hard to see why this Latino boy could build up a resentment against all white men based on this experience. The sad truth is that prejudice only begets more prejudice. It's unfair for the Latino boy to judge all white people from the actions of one person, but can you blame him? Moments like this create a cycle of unfounded anger that can produce significant racial divides. It muddles the distinction between acts born out of true racism and situations that are unintentional or taken out of context.

When it comes to the subject of biases and prejudices, we frequently point fingers and blame others. Interpretations of discrimination are rarely a one-way street. Every human interaction consists of multiple mindsets, assumptions, emotions, and biases from each individual involved.

Let's take for example the moment of the Latino boy again. Pretend the same boy, one week later, is walking down the same street, when a baseball hits him in the back of the head. He turns to see two white boys playing catch and assumes they threw the ball at him out of spite. Was this the case? Possibly. Or possibly not. One of the boys may have overthrown the ball and hit him by accident. When it comes to determining what constitutes a legitimate bias or prejudice, we cannot forget to factor in misunderstanding or human error.

Growing up in an extremely sheltered environment, I lived with a limited view of the world around me. If I didn't leave my bubble, I would never have experienced an expanded life or mindset. While I may have gained a wide spectrum of life experience by inhabiting other countries and immersing in other cultures, for a long time I vacillated between feelings of superiority and shame.

Even though I wanted to be accepted as just another person living in America, more often than not, it seemed that I was being viewed and treated differently as a Korean Asian-American woman. Compared to white students, I could feel a difference between us and could sense they were treating me differently. My other Asian and black friends felt similarly to me, which only compounded my feelings.

Every time I felt like I was being treated as a minority, I could feel a knot in my stomach, a sense of an unease. I didn't like to feel this way as it affected how I felt about myself. To my surprise, the moment people discovered that my father was an ambassador, everything changed. I was suddenly special and treated like a princess. I realized people were not seeing me for who I was; rather they were seeing an idea of me based on their own interpretation.

Through this experience, I learned that feeling biased or discriminated against is subjective. Unless there is a blatant offensive, my feelings of discrimination were largely a reflection of my own insecurities. For far too long, my sense of self was dependent on how I thought other people viewed me. I began to explore and adopt the stance that it was up to me to define who I was, not to subject my self-worth and self-image to others' unfounded assumptions. This revelation was pivotal in helping me navigate the complex emotions of being a minority in America. Just because I am a minority doesn't mean I have to feel less than anyone else.

It's impossible to know what someone else is thinking. There is nothing we can do about that, so we must remember that the only thing we can control is how we feel about ourselves. By becoming mindful of my own projections of how others viewed me, I started to interpret those around me differently. A skewed mindset is crippling because we start to assume all slights against us are intentional. While some may be, oftentimes we project our own biases onto others. Ironically, as a minority who has been stereotyped, my own projections of others' behaviors and thoughts can be equally stereotypical.

As others started to sense my comfort with myself, they too started to feel comfortable around me. Unconsciously, we project our own energy that is an amalgam of our sense of self. It is this energy by which others will view you. By changing the way that we feel about ourselves, we can change the space between ourselves and others. This is what healthy diversity is all about.

Making Progress with Bias and Prejudice

There seems to be an assumption that all biases and prejudices are primarily focused on race, skin color, and gender. This is a narrowly viewed assumption and only part of the truth. To illustrate, let's pretend that one thousand years from today every single race on Earth will eventually blend together as one, as scientists have already hypothesized. If every single person in this futuristic world was the same color, there would *still* be biases and prejudices. I imagine futuristic humans will find areas to discriminate, such as placing importance on bone structure, slight pigment differences, socioeconomics, or intelligence. The sad fact of life is that it is in our inherent nature to elevate ourselves by finding ways to push others down.

To state that we need to eliminate prejudice is a simplistic and unrealistic goal. This would be the equivalent of saying we must remove all anger from the world—a noble but impossible dream. We need to be honest about what makes us human, both the good and the bad. As we strive toward progress, we need to accept what is a virtue and what is a fallacy, what is realistic and what is idealistic. Our goal shouldn't be to *eliminate* biases; it should be to *reduce* biases by shifting mindsets and attitudes, working within the parameters of human nature. It is absolutely possible to expand empathy and goodwill within a society. It would be impossible, however, to expect a life free of biases and prejudices. Having a realistic mindset will allow us to view biases and prejudices with reduced anger, hostility, and hypocrisy.

Essential Takeaways

- Biases and prejudices are the powerful results of our rigid attachments to deep-seated beliefs. More often than not, we are unaware of our biased thoughts or actions. For example, viewing America's pervasive racial labeling as a bias might be a new concept because for years we've been conditioned to believe racial grouping is the foundation for diversity advancement. However, racial labeling leads to stereotyping, which builds biases, which in turn leads to racism. Undoing the unintended damaging effects of our actions or systemic processes requires a committed resolve to see and take steps to detach.

- We can't condone the actions of prejudices that discriminate; however, we also must accept the fact that having biases and prejudices is being human and universal. Acknowledging that it's almost impossible to remove ourselves from the provocations of biases and prejudices yet carry a humane and practical outlook would reduce the rampant anger, judgment, and accusation that fuel our divided atmosphere.
- There will always be those who accept differences with open arms, as well as those who are prejudiced. We can't change anyone else besides ourselves. When we are comfortable in our own skin, it's easier to navigate a world that is riddled with biases and prejudices. Self-empowerment diminishes the impact of external stimuli, thus expanding our capacity to connect and bring people together.

3

OUR LENS

A Bridge to Connection

Our lens is our story, the literal and figurative representation of the way we see and interpret the world around us. The lens reflects our mind and spirit, which dictates how we think, feel, and act. The lens's formation begins at birth, funneling the total of all our experiences, memories, insights, values, and beliefs. In many ways, the lens is hereditary—deeply impacted by our parents or caretakers' generational values and beliefs. It forms one's perspective, attitudes, biases, prejudices, passions, and relationships.

Who we are, who we were, and who we will continue to be depends entirely on the nature of one's lens. Just like our fingerprints, no two sets of lenses are the same. We see the same event and respond differently—this is one of the core drivers of conflicts and diversity challenges. One lens may be equipped with a wide angle. It may be adventurous, optimistic, and flowing with ideas and new possibilities. Another lens may be narrow. It may be isolating, static, pessimistic, and limiting. We live in a melting pot of diverse lenses, each unique and varying, that shapes the political, social, and diversity milieu we live in. Invisible to others, our lens guides how we see and act toward differences of color, size, shape, ethnicity, gender, etc.

Our lens can bridge connection or create separation. Every human being carries with them an energy that can either lift those around them or tear others down. Without exchanging a word, we have the ability to connect with those around us with the energy we emit through our lens. Energy is a transparent mirror of one's lens and one's emotional state. Whether we realize it or not, our energy is tangible and can be felt by those around us, both positively and negatively. Some lenses simply do not have the capacity to see and honor human differences. Without an open lens, we cannot have pervasive diversity.

The Lens that Defines Us

When I was growing up in South Korea, academic success was what defined a student's worth; this is still true today. This cultural mindset shaped my lens and the lens of the entire country. In truth, what we think we see is rarely the whole truth. If we only train to focus on certain aspects of life, such as academics in South Korea, then we fail to see the whole picture and miss the beauty that surrounds us. We see this in all cultures around the world, and within subcultures within those cultures.

When I attended middle school in South Korea before moving to Mexico City, all schools required students to wear badges on their uniform. Every morning, I made sure to have my badge, because if we didn't, we would be reprimanded. We had specific instructions on where to place our badge. For my school, the location of the badge was on the top-right corner of our collars, either on our school uniform blouses during the spring or on our jackets in the winter.

Each badge was specific to that school's emblem, so it was easy to identify where every student went to school. Although one might interpret this as a sign of school pride, it actually became a form of academic hierarchy. My badge didn't just represent where I went to school; it was a symbol that defined my intellectual achievement. Every school had its own reputation, and the badge reflected it.

Guess where my eyes went first when I encountered a new student I didn't recognize? To their badge, of course. If we glanced at students who went to a mediocre school, I'd immediately think less of them without a single interaction. From one look, I could size up where they went to school, how smart they must be, and if they were people I wanted to associate with. It felt good belonging to a school that was in such high regard. My badge bolstered my confidence, face, and sadly, my arrogance. As you can imagine, attending a top-ranked school was a major priority for Korean children and their parents, as it greatly impacted the entire family. You cannot imagine how much weight is placed onto children; their academic success or failure reflects not only on themselves but on their whole family.

Back when I was in South Korea, for each level of education (middle school, high school, and university), there was a highly competitive entrance examination. Unlike in the United States, where students apply to several schools using the same SAT or ISEE, this examination was good for one school. Schools were ranked, so each family determined the one school where they thought the child could make the cut. We had only one shot to make it into the school we chose. Across the country, all students took the same test at the same time in person at the school where they applied.

Under no circumstances could a student retake the test. If one was sick or couldn't arrive on time, they were simply out of luck. For those who failed the first round, there was a second-round examination reserved for second-choice schools (the top-ranking schools were not included). Retaking the examination was considered a failure and was a humiliating experience. And if you failed the second time, you had to wait until the next year; there was no third round. There were a few lower-rated schools in the outlying areas for those who failed twice. However, many students waited until the next year to retake the examination for the better school and spent the rest of the year studying. Therefore, when choosing the school of your choice, you had to pick wisely and go all-in on that one school.

While every family would have loved for their child to attend the best school in the country, if they didn't think the child had a realistic shot, they'd likely play it safe with a second-tier school. Think about the subliminal messages being sent to kids this early in life and how much these decisions could impact their life-long confidence. It's hard to explain the kind of pressure we experienced during this time.

To this day, I vividly remember all four hours of the examination, surrounded by other students who were just as nervous as I was, trying to get into the top-ranked girls' middle school. The examination was held in December, as the academic year begins in March in South Korea. As I recall, it was a very cold day and there were about three hundred multiple-choice questions covering every subject, with a cut-off of only thirteen wrong answers for my school. The following few days were terrifying as I waited to find out whether I had passed the examination. When I discovered I had gotten only five questions wrong, the relief I felt was enormous.

My school badge greatly impacted the formation of my lens that defined me and others. You have no idea the amount of pride I felt on the first day of middle school, and each time I put on my badge thereafter. I felt proud and respected when anyone took notice of my top-ranking badge. Although I wore the badge humbly, I couldn't help but feel superior to those who went to lower-ranked schools. Through an educational system built on ranking, Korean students learned to define a person's capability based on the badge they wore. Because of academic hierarchy, we rarely engaged with those outside our ranks. Our sense of pride turned into a form of arrogance and discrimination. Unknowingly, we were giving up opportunities to broaden our lens and to learn and connect with others.

Although that entrance examination system for middle and high schools was abolished in 1968, the academic pressure put on South Korean students has risen since. Today, great pressure is exerted on students to get into a prestigious university. On my recent visit to South Korea, I noticed that students start studying for college examinations at younger ages than we did growing up.

In South Korea, education has always been viewed as the main driver for social mobility. From the time I was seven years old, I remember being woken up as early as 6:30 a.m. to study before I went to school. Then, after school, I took additional tutoring in preparation for future academic success. At such a young age, most of my friends and I were already experiencing twelve-hour workdays, including Saturdays. Looking back, I don't remember having much time for play or extracurricular activities.

South Korea's zealous focus on education is well-known; the country's fast economic growth has been attributed to the importance it places on education. According to the Organisation for Economic Co-operation and Development (OECD), fifteen year olds in South Korea, among developed countries in the world, ranked second in mathematics and third in science.[1] The rigor of education instills discipline and work ethic at an early age, positive ingredients for growth and success. However, there are consequences of a high-pressure, all-work-and-no-play environment. Creativity and independent thinking are not nurtured nor encouraged under such a rigid education system. This pressure doesn't exist only within academics; it's instilled in the fabric of everyday society throughout one's entire life. This suffocation exerted on students is often cited as a key contributor to the country's high suicide rate. According to a 2017 *Berkeley Political Review* post, South Korea has the highest suicide rate in the world between the ages of ten and nineteen.[2]

Cultural environments shape the lens of the individuals who inhabit them, creating cycles of perpetuation. For example, politically speaking, urban and rural American communities often tend to lean toward progressive and conservative affiliations, respectively. Not only are urban and rural environments drastically different in appearance, but so are their values and day-to-day life. While one is not better than the other, we can understand how diverging ways of seeing the world ultimately lead to different directions one will take in life. From rural and urban America to South Korea, we can see the similarity in how cultural environments shape our lens and actions.

The Lens that Filters

In the late 1980s, I was hired as a marketing director for a major US health insurance company. My boss, a Southern gentleman, had a long career within the insurance industry and was extremely successful. He was a great manager and teacher. He took time to guide me into an industry I didn't know much about, and we had a very strong working relationship. One day about three months into my job, he suggested that I should enlist in English classes that could help eliminate my accent. He felt that my accent made me come across as an uneducated person, and that erasing it might help advance my career.

You can imagine the shock and pain I felt after hearing these words. After our meeting, I went back to my office and cried at work for the first time in my life. I was crying not because of his suggestion, but because of all the excruciating effort I had put in throughout the years trying to speak English properly. In one moment, all my hard work had been disregarded and my worst fears had become validated. Of course, I didn't think my boss was trying to hurt my feelings; he was just trying to be helpful. From his perspective, sounding like a native English speaker was an important attribute for any top executive. In this incident, my boss lacked the empathy to understand that many foreigners still have accents regardless of how long and well they speak another language. Through his lens, he was sharing his view of what qualities constituted a proper executive, and having an accent was not one of them. I often wondered why he hired me in the first place.

My English-speaking ability has always been one of my primary sources of insecurity. If it wasn't for the many compliments I've received over the years regarding my English, my boss's comments could have really hurt me. This situation taught me a powerful lesson: it is my responsibility to be open to the many lenses and various interpretations of others but to not let those define my own.

Years later, I took my children to a park with our new neighborhood friend Nancy and her three-year-old daughter, Jessica. The five of us were sitting around a picnic table, enjoying an afternoon snack. Jessica, who had never met me previously, quietly made a comment to her mother: "Mommy, that woman talks funny. How come she doesn't talk like us?" I immediately felt embarrassed for Nancy and was about to tell her not to worry about her daughter's comment. Instead, Nancy said something that I'll never forget.

With a smile, Nancy calmly explained to her daughter that English wasn't my first language and that "It's very hard to learn multiple languages. Isn't it great that Soo can do that?" Nancy continued to explain to Jessica that in the future, when she hears people speak with accents, it usually means that person knows more than one language and that it's not fair to assume everyone should speak English as naturally as they did.

Nancy's response touched me deeply, not only because of the way she opened her daughter's perspective, but because she was instilling Jessica's lens with acceptance and understanding for others unlike herself. What a beautiful and expansive lens Nancy had that she was now passing on to her daughter right before my eyes. What a difference Nancy's lens was from my boss's. Imagine if his mother had been like Nancy!

The Skewed Lens

One of my best friends, Zena, is a Jordanian single mother who was raised and educated in Jordan, Switzerland, France, the UK, and the United States. Zena raised two amazing sons, both born in the United States and brought up as Christians. As you can imagine, the three of them are invariably mislabeled as Muslims due to their Middle Eastern appearances and foreign-sounding names. Since the September 11, 2001, terrorist attacks, the boys have been stopped and searched "randomly" in airports on countless occasions.

Zena's youngest son, Hamza, has been a lifelong friend to my son since they were nine. Hamza is an outgoing, friendly, and caring young man who I consider a second son. Last year, while finishing college, Hamza was looking for a part-time job in northern Virginia. For several months, Hamza searched for any entry-level position he could find. He looked everywhere: restaurants, coffee shops, bakeries, retail, all to no avail. He filled out countless applications but never got a response, not one request for a single interview. Fortunately, a family friend knew a manager at a nearby Starbucks who was looking for a part-time employee during the busy holiday season. Hamza jumped at the opportunity and was soon offered the job. Hamza was delighted and accepted the position.

A few weeks into the job, a man ordered a coffee drink from Hamza during the holiday season. While Hamza was preparing the order, the man exchanged "Merry Christmas" greetings with other customers waiting in line. In a hurry to accommodate the many customers waiting in a long line behind the man, Hamza messed up the man's order by mistake and served him the wrong drink.

The man was livid. Hamza apologized profusely and corrected the drink order. Within a day, the manager received an email from the angry customer. The man wrote: "The Arab you have at the counter deliberately messed up my drink as an attack on Christians . . . your Arab was out to get me. . . ." The manager politely apologized for Hamza's mishap, offered the man a $10 gift card, and added that Hamza was a Christian, just like him.

In a flash moment, the angry customer interpreted Hamza through an Islamic-phobic lens. For all we know, this could have been a one-time instance or a regular occurrence. This man could have been anything: a great father, a good Christian, or an all-around jerk. Perhaps he was just having a rough week, or on the extreme opposite end of the spectrum, perhaps his wife was on one of the planes on 9/11. There is no way of knowing how this man came to have the lens he has, and I don't have an answer as to what could possibly expand his mindset for the future. It is presumptuous to make assumptions about other people's pasts or the mindset they carry. Nonetheless, skewed lenses can destroy human relations, hurting others in the process.

When a piece of information goes through our lens, that data is processed and interpreted within the scope of that individual's unique mindset; that information can then be reshaped and manipulated into something that was never intended. Many acts of discrimination are the result of subjective viewpoints that are falsely projected onto others. The same can be said for those who feel discriminated against when nothing malicious was ever intended. Unfortunately, people often act out because of their misguided interpretations of what they believe is the truth. From the angry customer's lens, he may have felt completely right in doing what he did. In his lens, he never considered the possibility that Hamza could have been a Christian or that the mixed-up order was an innocent mistake.

When we are triggered, whether by something real or projected, our reactions are predominantly driven by fear and anger. However, the need to retaliate shouldn't become the venue to vent one's projected assumptions. We must realize that our lens is our own and that there is an entire universe beyond what we know. If we can allow ourselves to think past our initial interpretations, we may be able to expand our lens and discover new truths from other perspectives.

Skewed Lenses Beget More Skewed Lenses

- "She is too emotional to do the job. He's aggressive and assertive. I know he can do the better job."

- "She has a family. She won't be able to travel as often. There's no way I can count on her the same way I can depend on him."
- "Be careful about hiring a minority, especially a black. It will take a mountain of paperwork to get rid of them when they don't perform."
- "Men will never help women. We have to break the glass ceiling."
- "All bosses are old white racist men. Some things will never change."

We've all heard phrases like these before. Skewed lenses that demean, belittle, and hurt people in unfair and unacceptable ways are a sad reality of the diverse world we live in. It is true: There are bigoted, racist, and hurtful people who want to keep others down in unfair and unjust ways. There are men who demean women in the workplace. There are stereotypes about women being inferior to men in the workplace and men being misogynistic toward women. There are people who racially profile and avoid hiring minorities.

Skewed lenses affect us all. I know many men, women, minorities, and majorities who are competent and many who aren't. Many who work hard and are open-minded, and many who resort to bitterness and unfair assumptions. There will always be people who care and strive for goodness. And there will always be people who carry biased and prejudiced mindsets and behaviors.

While this is a sad fact of life, it's equally unfair to presume that certain kinds of people all see through skewed lenses. Just because there are *some* old white men that are racist doesn't mean *all* old white men are racist. Just because *some* employers racially profile doesn't mean *all* employers racially profile. By making these kinds of assumptions about people with skewed lenses, we are acting no differently than those who have wronged others in the past.

Skewed lenses are nothing new. Kenneth Burke, a 20th-century American literary theorist, powerfully said: Men seek for vocabularies that are reflections of reality. To this end they must develop vocabularies that are selections of reality. And any selections of reality must, in certain circumstances, function as a deflection of reality.[3]

Falsely blaming our own failures on the skewed lenses of others means that *you* have a skewed lens. We must look before we leap. When we start from an inflexible stance or generalization, not only do we reduce the possibilities of seeing others beyond predetermined mental attitudes, we damage the opportunity to build productive and enriching relationships and connections. Most importantly, by making assumptions of others, we are only hurting ourselves by closing off the possibilities and benefits that having an open mind can bring us. It's easy to blame our failures on others, but we cannot let ourselves get lost in our lens and presume that anyone who doesn't agree or reward us thinks in skewed terms. That would be equally skewed and self-righteous.

You may ask: Is it possible for someone to know if they have a skewed lens? It's a case-by-case basis. Some people are so rigidly attached to their lens that they may be incapable of seeing outside of it. As a metaphor, I heard a news story about a man who refused to remove his daily contact lenses. He wore the same pair for more than a year. The lenses had become so ridged and crusty that he could no longer see. Eventually, doctors had to surgically remove them. I feel like this story illustrates the attachment that people have to their lens and their inability or refusal to see outside of it. If you cannot think outside of yourself, *you* may have a skewed lens.

The Lens that Stunts Potential

When my daughter was in elementary school, a prevailing bias that I encountered was that many mothers felt girls were genetically inferior in math and science as opposed to boys. Even in South Korea, an extremely male-driven society, I was raised with the mindset that there weren't many differences between boys and girls when it comes to intelligence. I have rarely met anyone in South Korea who thought there was a math and science impediment for girls.

With my daughter's elementary school friends' mothers, I strongly argued that having a propensity toward math or science has nothing to do with gender. My belief has always been that boys and girls are absolutely equal when it comes to intellectual capabilities. Aptitude is based on individual predispositions—some boys are better than girls and vice versa. They didn't buy my argument.

In America, I see that this biased mindset is still ingrained in many people. This may be one of the reasons why there are fewer females as opposed to males in the tech industry. The mothers' bias, without them realizing it, could have been silent seeds that deterred some young women from achieving their fullest potential.

Speaking of math and science, another prevalent bias I've noticed is that Asians are typically associated with having a natural proclivity toward these subjects. However, when you look at where industrial and high-tech innovations come from, in large part, they originated from the Western world. It's true that the Asian culture has a strong bias in favor of a highly structured and hierarchical educational system that focuses on quantitative strength over arts and creativity. The consequence of this rigid educational environment does not bode well when trying to nurture one's capacity to think outside of the box or excel as a unique individual. We don't see innovative powers like Bill Gates or Steve Jobs being produced in that system. Inadvertently, our biased lens can stunt our youths' potential when we could be nourishing them. Our biases cloud our lens and let us see only parts, not the whole.

The Lens that Limits Our Boundaries

We need to be cognizant of how differently others may view the world. Changing a lens cannot be forced; it must come from one's own volition. When managing global market research studies, I always enjoyed working with people with diverse perspectives. It was fascinating to observe my colleagues from different countries and cultures interpreting the same data in different ways.

It reminded me of a bedtime tale I heard growing up. In the story, there were three blind men who each touched a different part of the same elephant and described the animal very differently. One man, who touched the leg, said it felt like the column of a building; the other touched the skin of the elephant's ear, saying it felt leathery; and the third man felt the elephant's tusk, saying that it felt sharp. The blind men argued righteously, each claiming they were right and the others were wrong. They were all right and they were also all wrong.

It's hard to see a picture in its entirety unless we are willing to be open-minded about bringing together diverse insights and perspectives. This attitude is what healthy diversity requires. If we are open to bringing together our differences, we will reap collective knowledge that can paint a larger picture than any of us could have previously imagined.

The Lens that Channels Anger

Can you recall the last time you were furious? When you lashed out and lost control over your emotions? I know the feeling all too well. In the heat of the moment, emotions can erupt like a volcano and seize control of your mind and body. During these outbursts, it's almost impossible to regain control of what you are doing or what comes out of your mouth. When we see the world through our anger, we become blind to the impact of our actions. No matter how much we apologize afterward or regret what we did or said, irreparable damage has already been done and personal relationships may never be the same.

Anger is a core human emotion that we all possess. It is one of the main drivers of racial divides and diversity challenges. We live in a society that is mired in divisiveness and anger. Leaders today, in particular, who are fortunate to be in a position to inspire and shift public mindsets have a choice: to instigate further anger and separation, or advocate peace and unity. Ultimately, each of us is accountable for our own actions, no matter who is our leader. The ends do not always justify the means; actions that hurt or violate other human beings cannot be excused.

A lens that channels anger is a lens that does not see clearly; it clouds our thoughts and reinforces our skewed lenses with conviction. Anger is a powerful force that reflects the personal burdens one carries deep within. Like biases and prejudices, deep-seated anger builds up throughout one's lifetime. Every time there is a social injustice—for example, a police officer wrongly killing a black man, as we've seen many times—we see equally destructive riots that cannot be condoned as an appropriate response.

As Gandhi said, "An eye for an eye makes the whole world blind." By responding to anger with anger, we solve nothing and only make things worse. As a society, we need to continuously examine and re-establish clear consequences that denounce actions instigated by anger and hate. As individuals, we must be accountable for our own actions no matter how blinded we become through anger.

Learning how to manage one's anger deserves an entire book, but what I can say here is that it is possible to take control of your own emotions. While it may feel akin to regaining control of a car skidding on a rainy night, as long as we can become aware of the moment our car starts to lose control, we have the ability to change course and shift our direction. When it comes to controlling anger, I have a long way to go. A simple exercise that I find to be quick and practical is, in the heat of the moment, stop, take a deep breath, and feel your feet on the ground. This change in momentum works well for managing anger, fear, and nervousness. If we can become aware of our anger and the impact it has on others and on ourselves, we can start the process toward making lifelong changes.

The Lens that Shines Forgiveness

When I was living in Atlanta in the 1980s, I had the privilege of knowing Emma, a lovely woman in her mid-sixties who worked in a nearby deli. One day while I was at the deli, I struck up a conversation with Emma at the counter. She was so gentle and friendly. There was an indescribable spiritual energy about her that I was deeply drawn to. She mentioned that in addition to her work in the deli, she cooked dinners for small parties and families.

Because my husband and I were both working full time, we didn't have time to cook for ourselves. I thought it would be a treat for Emma to cook for us once in a while. So I invited Emma to our home for tea, and Steve and I asked her if she would cook for us once every two weeks, as that was all we could afford. Emma agreed and provided delicious, savory meals. She made the most delicious fried chicken I've ever had. I can still remember how Steve and I treasured her food. We loved Emma, not because of her fried chicken, but because of the loving energy she brought into our home, her company, and who she was.

During this time, my knowledge about black history in America was very limited. Although I was aware of slavery and the civil rights movement, I was by no means an expert on the subjects. Growing up in South Korea and Mexico City, these subjects were not a part of our curriculum. As an African-American woman, Emma was the first person to teach me about the segregation between whites and blacks, and how there were separate bathrooms, water fountains, and school buses. She taught me about how stores had signs out front that read "No Colored People" and how only help or servants were allowed into white establishments. I had no idea this kind of discrimination continued all the way into the 1960s and later. I didn't realize the full extent of how poorly black people were treated or how difficult it was for them to obtain well-paying jobs or gain social mobility.

What was astonishing to me was that while she was telling me her experiences of being discriminated against, Emma showed no anger or resentment. I asked her why she wasn't angry. I told her that if I was in her shoes, I could imagine anger reverberating throughout my body. Quietly and without the slightest tinge of hostility, she replied: "That was then. This is now. Times have changed. People have changed. I am happy that I no longer have to live under those circumstances. I am happy that the lives of my people are different now. What good would my anger do?"

I was blown away by her response. She was absolutely right. What good does holding onto past anger do? Emma taught me the importance of being able to forgive, no matter how horrible the past has been, and the power of being able to move on. If more people shared Emma's lens, regardless of race, I have no question that we would live in a much more collaborative and happy world.

Every day, we have the opportunity to either build connections or create walls, to move past anger or to succumb to it. Even if our present lens may be obstructive, we can choose to channel our love and empathy to broaden our lens. The way you choose to see and feel about yourself dictates the way you see others and how others see and interact with you. You are the master of your own journey; you are the only person who can adjust the direction and angle of your lens. At any moment, you have the power to change course, to steer out of the way of danger, and redirect yourself to greener pastures.

Essential Takeaways

- Our lens is a powerful factor in the way we participate, live, and work in diversity. We all possess unique lenses that guide what and how we see, how we interpret people, events, and situations, and the quality of relationships we build. Ultimately, our lens is responsible for fostering or polluting the diversity space in which we interact.
- At any time, we can choose to change and reshape our lens. By examining our lens without resorting to justifications, assumptions, projections, and blaming, we can begin to raise our awareness. Changes don't happen overnight and require taking mini steps.
- Self-examining your lens can help you learn and expand. Are you aware of the way your lens impacts your life and those around you? Are there aspects of your lens that you might want to reshape?

DIVERSITY
JOURNEY

4

MY JOURNEY INTO DIVERSITY

Feeling Different, Yet Similar

I was born in Busan the year before the Korean War ended in 1953. The city was poor and void of any modern advancements, quite the opposite of how it is today. Despite the economic conditions, the port city offered beautiful sandy beaches and abundant fresh seafood right out of the ocean. I have many fond memories of walking along the shore with my grandmother in the early morning, purchasing delicious fresh fish and seaweed from open-air markets. Thinking about the tasty fish soup my family enjoyed for breakfast in the wintertime, sitting around the warm ondol floor, fills me with nostalgia. On sunny summer days, my family would go to the beach. There, ladies would dive deep down into the sea, catch small abalones with their hands, shuck them, and walk down the beach chanting and singing "Fresh abalone, try my fresh abalone!" I loved those abalones and the delicious hot sauces the ladies sold with them.

Growing up with a South Korean general as my father, I was both proud and afraid of him. I remember flying in an army helicopter and getting motion sickness when I was only three years old. Instead of moving around with my father, my family lived with my mother's parents in their home that was attached to the hospital where I was born. My grandfather, one of the wealthiest men in Busan who later lost everything, practiced internal medicine. His house and the hospital together occupied an entire city block.

I was the oldest of four children, followed by two brothers and a baby sister. When I was eleven years old, before entering the sixth grade, my family and I moved all the way to Seoul, two hundred miles northwest of Busan, just so I could attend a top-ranked middle school. It may seem odd for an entire family to move to a different city for the sole purpose of advancing a child's middle-school education, but such things were not out of the norm in my country. Considering the country's devotion for education, my family's push for the best academics available exemplifies the culture. What was out of the ordinary was that my family moved on *my* behalf—a girl, not a boy. For generations, Korean culture has heavily favored men over women. Regardless, my parents wanted me to go as far as I could in life, for which I will always be very thankful.

Arriving in Seoul from Busan, I felt like a foreigner in my own country. Seoul has always been regarded as the most sophisticated metropolitan city in South Korea. When I first started at my new school, I felt out of place and much less sophisticated than my peers. Some of the students used to make fun of me because of my southern accent, which made me dread every time I had to speak or read aloud to the class. Even in a homogenous country such as South Korea, I still felt like an outsider, despite our identical race, skin color, culture, and language.

Seeing Differences as a Norm

In the late 1960s, my father was appointed the Korean ambassador to Mexico and Central America, which meant my entire family had to move to Mexico City. You cannot imagine how excited I felt about moving to the Western world, a place I knew nothing about.

Today, South Korea has the twelfth largest economy in the world and a population of more than fifty million people. However, in the 1960s, South Korea was one of the poorest countries in the world. There was very little in the way of automation; besides in the homes of the super wealthy, there were hardly any refrigerators, air conditioners, washers, or dryers, and very limited telecommunications. We seldom saw automobiles on the road other than military jeeps. Everything had to be done by hand, from washing clothes to daily cleaning. By moving to Mexico City, I broadened my view by being exposed to new ideas, environments, and people. Up to that point, all I knew was South Korea. I never realized that I was living in a poor country. We don't know what we don't know until we see and experience something different.

To build the country, the South Korean government restricted currency outflow and closed off imports from other countries. For us, Western goods were highly coveted, rare, and luxurious. There was a small black market for American goods, but with very high markups. For example, a large bag of M&Ms would cost approximately twenty US dollars today. The black market thrived in large part due to South Korean women who dated American servicemen. These women would smuggle goods from the US Army Post Exchange, hiding them in hollowed-out gourds underneath their clothing, pretending they were pregnant. It was amazing to see so many American goodies come out of their tummies.

During this time, it was extremely difficult to obtain visas to leave South Korea and travel overseas; only diplomats were able to do so. Because of my father, I found myself in a rare position. As a family, it was decided that we would all move to Mexico City. For the first time, I was leaving the only world I knew and entering into a vast ocean of differences and uncertainty that would change my life and perspective forever. Until then, in my universe, everyone looked Asian like me. How strange that I would soon be in a world where everyone looked different, yet through time, I would also learn how similar we all were.

When my family arrived in Mexico, we couldn't believe our eyes; Mexico City was far more advanced and modern than Seoul. At the supermarket, goods we could previously only buy from the black market were fully stocked on shelves for one-tenth of the price! You cannot imagine how excited we were to see all our favorites: Coca-Cola, M&Ms, SPAM, potato chips, and ice cream all at the tips of our fingers! It was amazing!

I started ninth grade at The American School, then the only English-speaking international school in Mexico

City. International children from all around the world attended The American School, as well as children of the wealthiest Mexican families. My classmates were an amalgam of all races, ethnicities, and accents. When I first started school, I was overwhelmed. Not only was I one of the few Asian students, but I hardly spoke a word of English. Up to that point, all I was accustomed to was Korean language and culture. Without question, my English-speaking ability was one of the worst in the entire school. My experience of feeling out of place when I first moved to Seoul from Busan was nothing compared to this. I felt like an alien from outer space trapped in the twilight zone. Not only did I look different from my classmates, I felt different.

When I first started school, I sat through my classes unable to comprehend anything. I could barely grasp a kindergartner's level of English, let alone Shakespeare and Chaucer. You can imagine how frightened and stupid I felt. Beyond the language barrier, the culture shock was even greater. I couldn't believe the way my fellow students interacted with our teachers. In South Korea, teachers commanded absolute obedience. Any time we encountered our teachers, whether on or off campus, we were expected to bow. There was an understood hierarchy that was never questioned. At The American School, students called teachers by their first names, an unfathomable notion to comprehend at first. What shocked me the most was when students put their feet up on their desks, right in front of the teacher, no less. I'll never forget walking through campus and seeing two students kissing passionately, out in the open for everyone to see! Public displays of affection were unheard of in South Korea. This was the first time I ever saw two people making out in public. Talk about feeling out of place!

As you can imagine, it was quite disorienting for me to assimilate into this new world. In a matter of a few months, I went from performing at the highest academic level in South Korea to not being able to complete basic homework assignments, even though I was working three times as hard. On top of just barely surviving academically, I had to find a way to bridge my Korean home life, my international school environment, and the Mexican culture simultaneously, all while catching up on my English. And I still had to maintain good standing with my family as the dutiful eldest daughter of an ambassador. That meant I had to be a role model for my siblings, my country, and family name at all times. At only fifteen years old, I felt a world of responsibility on my shoulders. In reality, I was struggling just to keep my head above water.

The most frustrating aspect of living in Mexico City was the fact that I wasn't allowed to freely mix cultures. On a daily basis, I was traversing between different mindsets and cultures. When I was at home, I was living in Korea. When I stepped out the door, I was in Mexico. Sadly, these two worlds never connected, and I felt like I wasn't able to fit into either one. My father forbade me from attending parties, sleepovers, and dating. I was allowed to play with girls my age, but never with boys. Growing up in South Korea, there was no such thing as co-ed parties between children. Beyond birthdays or family get-togethers, we never had any dances or mixers.

In Mexico City, I was invited to many co-ed mixers, but I was too afraid to ask if I could go. My father was very old-fashioned and believed it wouldn't be appropriate for a well-bred young lady to attend such things. I was dying to go but had to accept what I could not change. Secretly, my mother felt sorry for my predicament, so whenever my father was out of the country, she let me go. Every time I received an invitation, I prayed to God that my father would be out of town so I could attend. I hated having to make up reasons why I couldn't attend my friends' parties, too embarrassed to tell them the truth. I wasn't sure who I really was or who I should be.

As a teenager, I was having a difficult time coping with the changes thrown into my life, not to mention puberty and general teenage angst—both of which didn't even rank among my top ten personal problems at this time. Slowly, as my English started to improve, I started to feel more at ease and less like an outsider, and much less stupid. By strengthening my communication, I felt less awkward and more confident. Rather than sitting back and observing, I was finally participating as a member of the school community. I started to see and experience people and surroundings in a different light, and realized that everyone at The American School was just like me: completely different racially, culturally, and linguistically.

The American School community was a mixture of children from all over the world, almost a miniature version of the United Nations. I realized that being different was the norm and felt a weight lift off my shoulders. There were no labels, stereotypes, or categorizing of people based on race, skin color, or background. We interacted with the pervading underlying norm that the only difference among us was our names.

My classmates were genuinely interested in who I was. They wanted to learn about my background, what my life was like in Korea, and about my unique experiences. They weren't just making small talk; my new friends actually cared about me. Every student felt free to ask one another any question, without fear of unintentionally offending or being politically incorrect (at the time, there was no such thing). It was a priceless experience to be a part of an open environment in which our differences were embraced freely. This kind of openness allowed us to transcend differences and connect on a human level beyond borders and races. The American School's open atmosphere helped us to foster mindsets and attitudes that embraced and recognized our human similarities as opposed to our differences.

Whether we spend our entire lives in our own culture or in another that is foreign to us, we have as many similarities to others as we have differences. It doesn't matter who you are as an individual; we all share the same basic human needs and essences that connect us all to one another. In retrospect, The American School gave me a life-altering experience. Those four years provided the foundation that shaped the way I interact and see human beings. No longer did I see the differences in people; rather, I started to see the human beings behind the differences.

Coming to America

I came to the United States to attend college after my parents moved from Mexico City to London in 1971. This was the first time I was introduced to America. Like my move to Mexico City, this marked another major transition into a new world and culture. I didn't know it then, but this was the beginning of my life in the United States, the country I would ultimately call home.

Until this moment, my image of America was based on the few films I watched in Seoul. Watching Hollywood movies on the big screen—subtitled in Korean of course—was transportive and built up an enchanted image of America in my head. I'll never forget watching Audrey Hepburn in *Roman Holiday,* Elvis Presley in *Viva Las Vegas,* or my crush Sean Connery in *From Russia With Love.* Although *Roman Holiday* was filmed in Rome and James Bond is a British agent, to us, and to many other countries in Asia, anything that was Western—even if it was actually British or Italian—was synonymous with America. America was like the coolest kid on campus—more idolized and popular than anyone else—and we all wanted to be affiliated in some way. I used to cut out magazine clippings and make albums of my favorite Hollywood actors and actresses. I would swoon over Paul Newman, Gregory Peck, Cary Grant, and Roger Moore. Of course, the South Korean government censored all imported movies before they were released to the public, removing kissing or other intimate scenes.

The America I imagined in my head was a world populated with beautiful people like the actors and actresses I worshipped; an exciting new world full of romance, adventure, and wealth. Not only was America the land of movie stars and glitz and glamour, it also represented a land of freedom. Many foreigners come to America for opportunity; I came for freedom from the rigid rule of my father and Korean culture. I felt now, at last, I could do everything I wasn't allowed to do. I could finally start dating, go to parties, and stay out past 10 p.m.!

I was finally on my own in the country of my dreams, but I couldn't help but feel like a fish out of water. I came to America expecting to be treated with the same dignity, respect, and honor that I was accustomed to. Boy, was I wrong. Although I knew I was going to be a minority, I had no idea that I was not going to be seen as an equal. I don't know if this was because of the way certain people treated me or if I was projecting my insecurities of being different onto others; I think it was a little bit of both. "Oh! Where did you immigrate from?"; "You're so lucky to be here, aren't you?"; "Well, when are you going back home?" When you are frequently asked questions like these, it's hard not to feel like an outsider.

As a foreigner or as a minority, it's easy to feel as though there is a social stigma attached to us that provokes feelings of condescension and inequality. My nephew is one of these people. He is a smart, successful businessman working in South Korea, who has refused to move to America despite the many offers he has received to work here. My nephew attended both boarding school and college in the United States, so he is very well accustomed to US culture. Having lived in America for almost a decade, he has no desire to return because he cannot stand being labeled as a "minority" or to be treated better or worse than anyone else.

Being a minority in America, whether as a citizen or a foreigner, carries emotional baggage of feeling different and unequal. During his eight years in America, my nephew was always referred to as a "minority," which made him feel like an outsider—not to be included. There is a big difference between being a minority statistically and feeling like a minority emotionally. I can relate to how my nephew or anyone else in this situation feels. I wish there was one singular subject that I could point to that is cause of this issue, such as stereotyped labeling or a minority's mindset, but that would be an oversimplification of human dynamics.

I've spent a lot of time in this book demystifying labeling and addressing the unintended consequences of labeling and the human behavior behind it. Labeling is only a manifestation of one's narrowly defined lens. My hope is to expand our mindsets beyond limited boundaries. Whether we are dealing with diversity, labels, political correctness, interpersonal relationships, identity politics, or everyday conversation, confined thinking is the root for many of the causes behind our divisiveness and incompatibility to connect. To suggest one solution for any problem reveals the same core human mentality that also suggests using one label for any group of people. We must expand our mindsets so we can start thinking beyond labels and beyond singular solutions that limit our capacity to connect and grow.

Superficial Eyes

During my four years of college, I shuttled between Baltimore and London. Not only was I moving between two different countries, I was also moving between two different identities. In America, I was a foreign student from Asia; in England, I was an ambassador's daughter. As you can imagine, within the same day, I could be treated as royalty in one place and as no one special in the other.

This experience taught me how quickly people make snap judgments about others based on superficial interpretations. We often see people as what we assume them to be, regardless of any concrete substance or truth. When I traveled between these two countries, nothing about who I was changed. I was always Soo; the only difference was the image people had of me. It was amazing how people's interpretation of me was based on an image they saw, not the content of a person. This superficial view of a person is a driving force of biases and discriminations—a snap judgment of a person based on race, class, or immigration.

While I was traversing between two extreme worlds, my sense of worth was in constant flux. In the years after college and even after I became a naturalized US citizen, these feelings stayed with me as long as I traveled back and forth. I slowly realized that I was becoming as shallow as those people who viewed me. I was placing too much importance on outside reinforcement. I loved being seen as an ambassador's daughter because that meant I was no longer seen as a minority, even though neither image defined my being. A sense of belonging can come only from within, not from the outside.

Eyes that See Differences, Hearts that Feel Similarities

During my college years in the United States, I always looked forward to getting together with my girlfriends. The main topic of our gossip was our weekend dates. Going on dates was exhilarating but also terrifying. I was going against the norms of South Korean culture, a world where the daughters of so-called good families found their husbands through arranged marriages. I was afraid that I might be seen by another Korean on my dates, who would then tell my family or other Koreans, who would then spread rumors and ruin not only my chance of marriage, but also the reputation of my family. This was hysterical thinking, but I would be lying if I told you that these thoughts didn't cross my mind on every date. I mentally calculated the time difference between Baltimore and London every time I went out on a date, just in case my father called me while I was out.

My college didn't allow private phones in our dorm rooms until we were juniors. In the meantime, my entire floor shared one hall phone. If you think the line for the women's bathroom is long, you've never had to wait for the phone in my residency hall. Before a date, I would knock on every room on my floor and instruct my friends that if my father called, tell him I was studying in the library. Lucky for me, my father rarely called on weekends. I felt incredibly self-conscious about constantly having to cover up to my parents. I was afraid that everyone thought I was a weirdo. There were other girls who seemed sheltered or overly dependent on their parents, but my case was different. It wasn't my parents I was abiding by, it was my culture, and no one understood the rules other than me. Even when I would explain, I would get only blank looks; it was out of the realm of my American friends' reality.

After my dates, almost invariably, my friends would ask me, "What color were his eyes?" or "What color was his hair?" At first, I didn't know how to answer them because I had absolutely no idea. I didn't pay attention to my date's eye or hair color because those distinctions never crossed my mind before. It may sound absurd, but unless I saw drastic characteristics that really stuck out to me, I didn't pick up on these things. I'm sure I would have registered a man with blue hair if I met one, but I didn't notice the difference between dark brown, light brown, or black hair. However, what I did remember about my dates were their facial features, their posture, and their personalities. Influenced by my girlfriends in the United States, I tried to pay attention to traits such as hair and eye color but still had difficulty seeing them.

The way my girlfriends and I saw our dates was based on our conditioned mental framework. I came to the realization that my own focus was heavily influenced by the homogenous society in which I grew up. In Korea, we weren't attuned to color differences because everyone had dark brown eyes and black hair. Instead, Korean culture focuses more on facial structure and alignment.

To this day, there are professional face readers in Korea who devote years of study to learn how to read people's faces. Certain features meant certain predispositions or predictors of a person's destiny. For example, it is said that women with visible gum lines when they smile will be widowed early. Another superstition states that the flatter the indentation between one's nose and mouth, the less likely the person will be blessed with children. As silly as these things sound, these facial characteristics were not taken lightly, and they influenced marriages and employment. Another Korean superstition was that females with high cheekbones would not have an easy or pampered life.

Unfortunately for me, I have high, prominent cheekbones. Whenever my grandmother had the chance, she would push her fingers into my cheekbones, hoping they would get smaller. I was relieved when I found out that high cheekbones was considered an attractive feature in America! These centuries-old beliefs are still embedded in South Korean culture, and I haven't escaped them. After fifty years of Western living, I still catch myself staring at people's faces, wondering what correlations can be made between their features and their lives. It is amazing how resistant to change our deeply rooted beliefs are and how greatly they influence our perspectives. These kinds of thoughts wouldn't even occur to Americans, as they are way outside of American culture.

Despite our differences in our focus and way of life, my girlfriends and I all wanted the same things. We talked into the wee hours sharing our hopes, aspirations, fears, and spirituality. We took care of each other. While our cultures and outlooks may have varied, our hearts were connected by our core humanity. After all, we weren't that different.

A Foreigner Within

Looking back today in my mid-sixties, I realize that I lived for many years as a foreigner to myself. I am using the word *foreigner* here both literally and metaphorically. Living as a foreigner within is a state of mind that has no bearing on one's upbringing or culture; you don't have to be a foreigner to feel like a foreigner within yourself. It all comes down to the self-image you carry and the way you feel.

Caught in between two extremely different cultures of East and West, between being the daughter of a prominent family and being an immigrant in a foreign country, I struggled to find my identity. I was an outsider navigating new worlds while also feeling like a foreigner to myself. My connections to others mirrored the disconnect I felt within. Rather than being comfortable with myself, I projected a facade of what I thought people expected of me. If I couldn't feel connected to myself, how could I expect others to connect with me?

Becoming comfortable with who you are is a lifelong journey. It took me many years before I was able to feel confident in my own skin. For a long time, it mattered to me that I didn't fit in, that I didn't speak English flawlessly, or that I was labeled as a minority. I placed too much importance on what others thought of me and the things that I couldn't control. Once I started to let go of the things I couldn't control (my accent, my background, my race), I started to become much more empowered. I started to love who I was, and accept the blemishes that I couldn't control, rather than beating myself down because of them. Having a sense of inner harmony is what connects me with myself and to others. I may not be able to control how others label me. All I can do is focus on being Soo.

Oftentimes, I see people trapped within themselves, unable to connect to themselves or others. How one views oneself in comparison to others (feeling more than, less than, higher than, lower than, different than, etc.) can trigger feelings of self-doubt and confusion. Possessing a grounded sense of self is a universal struggle we all face regardless of race, background, or culture. Once we start to look past labels and stop trying to live up to projected images of who we think we should be, we can then begin to build connections to our true selves.

Despite having lived in the United States for forty-nine years, I still may be considered a foreigner. Yet, in many ways, the idea of living in South Korea is even more foreign to me. For a long time, I didn't feel at home in either South Korea or the United States. I existed in a no-man's land, somewhere in between, a sentiment with which many immigrants can identify. You could say the same thing about how my mind used to function, operating between two modes of thinking.

Crossing through a multitude of cultures and mindsets, I learned that regardless of how different we look on the outside, we are far more similar than we realize. Think about the two-thousand-year-old tales of Aesop, a slave and storyteller from ancient Greece. Regardless of language, culture, race, or geographical boundaries, Aesop's tales have been shared and translated all around the world for centuries, evoking the same universal human emotions that connect us all. As a child in Korea, I learned about the story of the tortoise and the hare, just as my husband had learned about it when he was growing up in America. The fact that Aesop's work has been understood and shared around the world since the sixth century BC is a testament to how connected we truly are.

Everyone on this planet wants healthy relationships with loved ones, friends, and colleagues; parents share the joy and challenges of raising children; and we aspire to have a fulfilling life and career. We also share the same fallacies: insecurities, jealousy, greed, righteousness, and ego. I learned that human connection is bridged over similarities, not differences. This orientation opens my eyes and heart to a sense of belonging. I don't distinguish myself as a Korean, an American, an Asian, an immigrant, or a minority; I feel connected to myself and to others as a person, no longer as a foreigner within.

Essential Takeaways

- Notwithstanding our differences, we each share a universal human essence regardless of who we are and what cultures we come from. Through humanity, we build harmonious acceptance; a connection that transcends external differences. Forwarding perspectives and measures that embrace human elements will shift the diversity paradigm to a new place where we honor human similarities over differences.
- Having a sense of belonging is a driving force for advancing diversity and inclusion. While differences are a fact of life, feeling different is evoked by one's inner world based on history and social experiences. The less we are impacted by a sense of feeling different, the greater we feel a sense of belonging.
- Beliefs, actions, and programs that accentuate differences, such as racial labeling and grouping, inadvertently amplify people's feelings of being different. By doing so, we take away opportunities to create a connecting space. Attaining a sense of belonging is also very much an individual's effort. Owning a strong self-identity goes hand in hand with one's sense of belonging.

5

INDOCTRINATION OF EARLY SCRIPTS

Shaping the Self

I recall it vividly; it was a beautiful sunny spring day and I was only five years old. I peeped through a narrow crack between the two massive wooden gates that enclosed our home. Occupying nearly the entire block, our house was one of the largest in the city. With my little body stuck to the gates, I could hear and partially see the neighborhood children laughing and playing just outside. Unable to leave my home, I daydreamed about what it would be like to play with the other children.

I gasped. My father, a military general, sprayed me from behind with the full force of a water hose. "How stupid can you be to put your eyes up to that crack? Those kids could have poked your eyes out with a stick! You're not like those other children," he admonished. Hurt and afraid, I began to sob, which only annoyed my father further. Even at five years old, I was taught that well-mannered children did not cry and that crying in public was shameful. Regardless, I could not stop the tears. I was scared that I'd provoked my father's anger, but perhaps more upset that my brand-new outfit had been soaked and ruined. I still remember that outfit: a pair of blue capri pants with a matching white short-sleeve shirt. My aunt rushed out into the garden and took me into the house away from my father. Instead of providing sympathy, my aunt scolded me for my inappropriate conduct.

I only vaguely understood why my father was punishing me. I was forbidden to mingle with the children outside because they were not considered to be from good homes. But what did that mean to me? In my mind, I was one of them and they were just like me. However, the cold shower my father inflicted on me as a five-year-old child has had a long-lasting impact on me. After that day, I no longer looked out through our gate or thought about playing with the other children. Instead, I was petrified to ever do such a thing again. I started to believe that I was separate from the children outside and that they may poke my eyes out. As the years passed by, I started to believe the scripts that were instilled into me at an early age. I began to believe that I was not like the others, that I truly was superior.

Indoctrination to early scripts is a formula that shapes every one of us. I am using the term *script* as a way to describe all the things that we soak in at an early age from our specific environments. Socioeconomics, beliefs, culture, religion, time, and place are variables in that universal equation.

My early script impressed upon me the idea that I belonged in a superior social class. Ironically, years later after the water hose incident, my destiny would take me to America, where I would live as an Asian immigrant. There, I felt a great sense of inferiority due to my lack of English fluency and my minority status. Having experienced both polarities, I learned that the feeling of superiority and inferiority are no more than states of mind. It's amazing how a mental status can become a mental trap. When statuses become self-beliefs, that's when we fall into a false reality or self-image.

Throughout history, the foundation of all discrimination, racism, and fear-driven control stems from the power of inferiority and superiority. Oppressors feel superior and will make sure that those who they oppress remain feeling inferior. When someone feels inferior, they allow themselves to be walked on. The battle of racism and discrimination is a mental war, not a physical one.

The scripts we identify with dictate the way we see the world through our lens and the way we think and feel about ourselves and others. And these scripts can shift throughout one's life. Like an NFL quarterback, we have the ability to call an audible and change the script whenever we choose; all it takes is the power to realize that we can be the quarterback in our own lives.

Generational Imprints

How often do you hear yourself saying, "I am nothing like my parents" or "Oh God, I'm just like my parents!" Even though we may not want to believe that we are anything like our parents, often we are different sides of the same coin. Scripts transfer between generations. It's easy to underestimate how much we inherit from our parents (or caretakers), and from their parents before them. The cycle will continue with us unless we find a way to change it.

To illustrate this point, I'll share the story of a close friend—let's call her Leah—who is liberal and proudly left-wing. Her father, a man I know quite well, is conservative and right-wing. While they couldn't be more different in ideology, their behaviors are almost identical. Her father is righteous, unwilling to hear other perspectives, and can come across as offensive to others because of his uncompromising demeanor. The same exact thing can be said about Leah.

Imprints of My Father

My father was born in 1920 in the southern-central region of Korea, while it was under the rule of Imperial Japan. His father was a terrible alcoholic and a well-to-do landowner in a small town. Upon his mother's request, every evening since the age of eight, my young father was sent out in the middle of the night to retrieve his drunken father from a local pub far away, across a heavily wooded forest. As my father recounted his experience, he told me how scared he was, walking alone through the pitch-black woods, hearing the sounds of crying wolves and whistling trees. Every inch of my father's body shook in cold sweats. Rather than being happy to see his young son, his father beat him when he arrived at the pub.

During my father's youth, Korean culture placed a major emphasis on the importance of the first-born son. While boys were valued far more than girls, any boy born after the first-born was not considered as important. My father was born second in a family of six children: three boys and three girls. By virtue of being born second, my father's birthday was never celebrated. He was forced to do all the chores, while the first-born son didn't have to do a thing. Even today in the 21st century, a small number of old-fashioned Korean fathers still consider the first-born son to be more important, often passing on all the family rights and inheritance to them.

My father was a bright student whose childhood ambition was to be a teacher, the most respected profession at that time. His mother knew her young son was gifted and felt he was destined to live a life of significance. She wanted to provide him a path to blossom, yet she was helpless for not knowing how. This was during the Japanese colonization of the Korean peninsula that lasted from 1910 until 1945, when Japan was defeated in World War II.

Japan ruled with an iron fist and tried to integrate Korea into the Japanese Empire by assimilating Koreans into Japanese language, culture, and the Shinto religion (the divinity of the Emperor). Koreans were forced to speak in Japanese and adopt Japanese names. The Japanese discriminated against Koreans and viewed us as an inferior race. Many Japanese called Koreans *josenjing*, meaning the people of the Joseon dynasty of Korea (1392–1910) prior to the occupation. The word carried a derogatory connotation that depreciated Koreans.

The oppressor's message became part of my father's early script, that Koreans were inferior to Japanese. For the rest of his life, the scripts that the Japanese had imparted into my father enforced the idea that he was never good enough. Relentlessly, my father spent the rest of his life trying to prove his worth to himself—a desire that would never be attainable. His sense of self was created by a false notion that he adopted without question, which is a sad reality that many of us can relate to.

For my father, an opportunity presented itself that would change his life forever. At the age of twelve, he was selected to go to Japan to a foster family. As a strategic tactic to further assimilate Korea, the Japanese government selected the best and the brightest young Korean boys and brought them to Japan to indoctrinate them as their own. The Japanese excluded first-born sons in order to avoid public outrage. The goal of this program was to educate, assimilate, and groom young Korean boys into the Japanese culture and mindset so that they could eventually be sent back as leaders to their own country under Japanese rule. While in Japan, my father studied hard, followed all the rules, and took on responsibilities to show the Japanese that he was competent and worthy of their respect.

After living in Japan for thirteen years, my father returned to Korea soon after the liberation of his country on August 15, 1945. He was twenty-four years old. It was a time of confusion and turmoil for Korea, brought on by sudden social and political changes. Even though my father didn't share much detail about his early years in Japan, it wasn't hard to grasp the complex mixture of emotions he carried living as a *josenjing* in Japan: anger, fear, shame, loneliness, and desire for approval.

Upon his return, he decided to pursue a military career by joining Korea's fledging army. My father's rise within the army was swift. As a young general, he fought in the Korean War, almost losing his life several times. He suffered major injuries, including eight gunshot wounds.

As a young child, I used to stare in terror at the large gunshot scars on his arms and legs. My father would eventually rise to become the chief of staff of the Republic of Korea Army as a three-star lieutenant general (three-star was the highest military rank at that time).

My father lived a tumultuous and complex life. He served his country in many ways: as an ambassador, as a Cabinet minister, and as a member in Congress. Despite all his accolades and accomplishments, he never felt satisfied by his achievements; no matter how great they were, he always thought they could have been better. My father was never able to knock the chip off his shoulder that the Japanese had inflicted on him. While the occupation was long over, his rigid attachment to false scripts remained. His pursuit of excellence was relentless.

There were many life principles that he drilled into me and my siblings, including honesty, integrity, and compassion. However, there were two principles that may have done more harm than good: "Always work hard and never stop striving to reach the top of everything you do" and "When you accomplish something, whether big or small, enjoy it for a moment, but never relax. The moment you relax, you will slide all the way to the bottom." Both of these messages are exhausting and impossible to achieve. In this sense, I always felt I was never good enough, just like my father.

I idolized my father despite his many shortcomings. Even though he wasn't much of a drinker, my father carried the same unpredictable temper that his alcoholic father had, and that kept me and my siblings terrified. My father's mindset and messages have continued to echo inside of me throughout my life. My heart went out to my father for the hardships he'd endured, even as I unknowingly adopted many of his destructive patterns and beliefs.

By placing my father's messages on a pedestal, I didn't realize how devastating they were to my mental and physical well-being, as they must have been to him as well. Even worse, I preached the same messages to my children just as my father preached them to me. Very early in my children's formative years, I did my best to pass on my father's ideology and work ethic. I relentlessly pushed my children to be the best, just like I was told. I made sure they had early tutoring and early SAT and SSAT prep (an application for high schools), and we talked early about prestigious high schools and colleges to attend. Early everything with the expectation of excellence and nothing short of it.

In my mind, I was doing what any good parent would do, regardless of how much stress and anxiety I was inducing. Of course, my parenting style was unsustainable and unhealthy. I started to notice how much anger and frustration both my children had built up inside. Worst of all, I sensed a lack in confidence from my children. It was damaging to set the bar so high; when my children didn't achieve, they felt like failures. Without realizing it, I became my father. My father lived his life petrified of failure, I lived my life petrified of failure, and now my children share the same inheritance.

Our positive and negative imprints stick in our brain and heart in a powerful lasting manner. It's not about getting rid of all the hindering imprinted traits—an impossible feat being human. Rather, it is about becoming less affected by them.

Imprints of My Mother

My mother was born in Busan, the largest city on the southeastern-most tip of the Korean Peninsula, eight years after my father. Her father was one of the wealthiest men in the city. In stark contrast to my father's alcoholic father, my maternal grandfather was a very loving man who spoiled his four children with his big heart.

Until she was seventeen years old, all my mother knew was the Japanese language and culture. As it was mandated, she was given a Japanese name as well. In comparison to my father, my mother's experience of the Japanese occupation was very different. While my father, living in Japan as a Korean, felt the brunt of the discrimination and oppression inflicted onto Koreans, my mother, like many of her contemporaries, generally had a pleasant experience living in Japanese-occupied Korea. Their distinctive experiences reveal how varying degrees of human experience can occur under similar conditions, leaving entirely different imprints. The same can be said about influence within the same household. How can children raised from the same two parents be so different from one another?

My mother's scripts differed greatly from my father's. Rather than pushing her children to the top, she accepted us for who we were. She didn't instill a "life-or-death" fear of failure mentality and wasn't as judgmental as our father. She was open, and I felt as though I could share almost anything with her, a trait I can happily say I've transferred to my own children and their relationship with me.

After I passed a stressful and difficult examination that got me accepted into the top girls' middle school in

South Korea, my first report card was abysmal. For more than a year, I worked my butt off doing everything I could to get into that school. But once I was in, I simply could not maintain the same rigorous discipline. When I was first accepted, I entered my class in the top 10 percent academically. My first report card put me in the bottom 10 percent. The school required a parent's signature for all report cards and I dreaded sharing the horrible news with my parents. There was no way I was going to be able to show that card to my father and live to tell about it. Ultimately, I picked my poison and ended up sharing the report card with my mother.

I remember dragging my feet on my way to present her with the report card. She reviewed it calmly; then after what felt like an eternity she quietly said: "I understand you must be burnt out after being pushed so hard for so many years. Promise me you will think about this, learn from your report card, and return to being the great student I know you are. I trust you."

This was a solemn and poignant moment that marked my first glimpse into the enormity of the meaning of the word *trust.* I may not have realized the depth of the word then, but my mother's trust gave me an indescribable feeling of responsibility and empowerment. In so many ways, my mother acted as a neutralizer to my father's harsher scripts in the shaping of who I am today. Yet she also carried a sense of arrogance as though she was superior to others, as well as traits of being spoiled. Neither of my parents were above human imperfection.

Due to my father's prestige and stature, I always felt he was larger than life. Naturally, I gravitated to him and believed his influence on my life was more significant than my mother's. The reality is that the scripts we inherit are multidirectional. Many people claim that they take after one parent over the other, but the fact is that we are a subconscious blend of both. Not until later in my life did I truly grasp the power of my mother's influence on me. Just because one script appears softer than the other doesn't mean it's less impactful.

No One Escapes Generational Imprints

As children, we don't have the wherewithal to question what is presented to us. We subconsciously assume the beliefs and values of our families and our environments. Unbeknownst to us, our past dictates the way we focus on the present and future. I often wonder what my life would have been like under a different script, if I were raised just like the children outside of my gate. I may not have grown up with the skewed perspective that I was superior to the other children. Was my father a bad person for instilling his harsh scripts into me? Absolutely not. My father possessed numerous virtues that I loved and looked up to him for. And he also possessed many human limitations. Yes, his admonishing actions were reactive, blunt, and severe. But in his mind, he was protecting me from potential danger. He thought he was educating me about and making me aware of the boundaries of separation. These were his fears, not mine. In return, an intangible wall of separateness, distrust, and fear about the outside of my insular world was being instilled in me.

In one way or another, we all are bound by the burdens of our generational imprints. Their tentacles spread deep and wide, and those scripts dictate our mindsets and actions. The way we build our own imprints from the scripts we inherit is not always straight and narrow. We are not mirror images of our parents, but rather an impressionistic collage of beliefs, mannerisms, attitudes, biases, and everything in between.

What we witness in others is the result of their own inner workings shaped by the scripts unique only to themselves. We all come with different scripts that we didn't have control over. It would be rash to judge or denounce anyone who does not align with our own thinking and behaviors. At the end of the day, no one is above their early scripts or their lasting imprints. Looking at life from this angle may help us expand our empathy for those with divergent mindsets and attitudes.

Essential Takeaways

- We each walk our own diversity journey shaped by our early scripts. There is no such thing as a right or wrong path. Opening up to the bumps we experience along our path can help us get acquainted with how we've become our present self. Empathy and reflection can give us a glimpse into a new direction.
- By embracing the complex dynamics that formed our lens and mindsets, we can begin to see and accept ourselves with a broader understanding. This in turn helps us see others in a new light. Acceptance does not have to be an endorsement. However, accepting others no matter how they may be can help navigate our world without impulsive anger and judgment of others.

6

DEMYSTIFYING CULTURAL DIFFERENCES

Coming Together

We live in a world that is getting smaller every day. As our world slowly melds together, our contact with diverse cultures increases. What connects us is not knowledge or exposure; connecting is about embracing our shared humanity and respecting everyone as an equal human being. Through shared humanity, we can see the commonalities among all people regardless of language, culture, or physical differences. When we peel away cultural differences, we discover universal human traits and behaviors that transcend borders and races.

Cultural Bias

For as long as I've known, many South Koreans seek the advice and guidance of fortune-tellers. Every single fortune-teller predicted the same thing about me: I was going to marry a Westerner and live in America. In Asia, the term *Westerner* commonly refers to a white individual from Europe or North America. My grandmother and mother were deeply saddened by the fortune-tellers' predictions and never uttered a word to my father. For a Korean woman, especially one from a prominent family, marrying a Westerner was considered one of the worst acts a woman could commit.

Woven into the fabric of our mindset was the belief we were never to marry outside our race or class. Originally stemming from China, this belief has been embedded into many Asian cultures for centuries. Believe it or not, the father of a Japanese friend of mine ended up in the hospital with high blood pressure after discovering his daughter was going to marry an American. During the Korean War, most of the women who were seen with American soldiers were prostitutes. This stereotype stuck, and after the war, the perception of women who associated with Western men grew worse. At best, they would be looked at as a slut, at worst, a prostitute.

I met my husband, Steve, at business school during the early 1980s. Despite our cultural differences and my deep loyalty to my family, Steve and I quickly fell in love. This unintentional act of defiance was not only seen as a cultural betrayal, it could have ruined my family's reputation and face within South Korea, especially my father's. Because he was a highly respected figure, if the public found out that a Korean leader's daughter was marrying a Westerner, it would have been a major blow to his public image. I felt my actions were selfish and I also worried about the potential to negatively impact my brothers' and sister's prospects of marriage. In order to maintain the face of the family, it was customary and crucial that my siblings and I were to marry into an equally respectable Korean family. By marrying an American, my actions had the potential to tarnish my entire family's reputation, as I would have been labeled as a corrupted and promiscuous woman. For a long time, I legitimately thought I had a brain tumor from all the emotional turmoil and headaches I was experiencing from being split between two worlds.

Steve and I got married shortly after graduating from business school. At that time, my father was the Korean ambassador to Japan and lived in Tokyo. My parents refused to accept or even acknowledge our relationship, and as you can imagine, they did not attend the wedding. By choosing a life with Steve, I had turned my back on my family. While I had a small sliver of hope that my parents might still accept our marriage, I still was deeply saddened by their decision to not attend. Nonetheless, I accepted the consequences of my actions and knew full well that I was going against my cultural norms and expectations.

A few years after the wedding, I learned that my father had all of my photos removed from inside their home. Far from being outraged by my parents' lack of support, I was grateful they didn't disown me completely. Despite my father's love for America, he couldn't accept my marriage to an American. Like our emotions and religions, cultural allegiance cannot be explained through logic.

Despite everything that happened, I still loved my parents deeply and became very homesick. Although I was the black sheep of the family, I was still invited to visit my parents in Tokyo; my husband was not. When I went to visit, no one within the embassy knew I was married. They would say to me, "You should marry before you get too old." I would smile and nod, laughing bitterly to myself. To those who didn't know my secret, I was an attractive eligible bachelorette, an ideal partner for upper-class South Korean men. I politely turned down constant offers and played along while I deceived everyone, including myself.

Visiting my parents in Tokyo was one of the strangest times in my life. On one hand, I loved being re-embraced by my family and being accepted. One the other, I was living a lie. It was painful to know that my parents still loved me but could not accept me or my husband. There was an inner friction and pain that pulled me between my loyalty to my husband and to my family. I hated lying to everyone and not being truthful about Steve, not to mention the resentment he must have felt. While he understood that he could not come with me to Japan, I could tell he was hurt. Fortunately, my husband and I have a wonderfully candid relationship and mutual support for our extreme differences in cultures and backgrounds. Despite Steve's generous heart full of love and empathy, I felt perpetual guilt over what I was putting him through.

After I returned to our home in Atlanta, I called my mother and asked if I could bring Steve to Tokyo but keep him out of sight of the Korean embassy staff. I suggested that we could go to a hotel directly from the airport and that they wouldn't have to send out a car for us. This way, my father could come to our hotel room without anyone knowing and meet my husband in person for the first time. My mother had already met Steve in Hawaii a few months after we got married, but my father never did. I was confident that once my father met my husband, he would get over his bias and finally approve of him.

My mother was hesitant, but told me she'd ask my father. I anxiously awaited my mother's call, and hoped that she was able to persuade my father to follow my idea. A few days later, I eagerly picked up her phone call and found out that his answer was no. I was crushed but understood the reality of the world I lived in.

A few years later, we gave birth to our first child, Sophia. Secretly, my father was dying to see his new granddaughter and finally invited our entire family to come visit. This would be the first time in our six-year marriage that my father would meet Steve. By this point, my parents had moved back to their home in Seoul. As my father's daughter, the prospect of being seen with an American man gave me deep feelings of angst and shame. While my twenty-month-old daughter cried throughout the entire fourteen-hour flight, all I could think about was the first meeting between Steve and my father. Thoughts swirled in my head. What if they didn't get along? What if my father felt ashamed of being in public with us? What if my father wanted only to see my daughter and ignored my husband? Despite my excitement for my husband to finally meet my father, I was afraid of what emotions might be trigged inside Steve after more than six years of rejection. I prayed that it wouldn't be a disaster.

Once we landed, my father's driver picked us up and brought us to my parents' home. We got out of the car and nervously walked up the stairs, knocked on the door, and waited. My father opened the door and as I had specifically instructed Steve, we bowed down per our cultural etiquette. Politely, my father shook my husband's hand, welcomed us inside, and eagerly asked to hold my daughter in his arms. The rest of the day was pleasant, but I feared a breakdown might occur at any moment. Surprisingly, my father and Steve got along well and even played golf together! I didn't know how to read the situation, whether it was authentic or a facade. It wasn't until that evening when I realized how my father truly felt.

That evening, the whole family went out to a nice dinner at a well-known hotel. For the first time, my parents, my brothers, their wives and children, my sister, my husband, my daughter, and I were all together; it was surreal. As we were leaving the hotel, my father carried Sophia in his arms. The doorman, who recognized my father from public media, bowed deeply. When he lifted his head up and saw my daughter, his eyes grew wide. To Koreans, half-Asian, half-white people only look white, as my children can tell you from firsthand experience. The doorman's expression was priceless, and I had to do my best to not laugh out loud. The doorman did not expect my father to have a half-white granddaughter.

My father looked the doorman in the eye and proudly said, "This is my granddaughter, isn't she beautiful?" This touching moment brought tears to my eyes. I will forever carry this moment in my heart knowing my father's love for me transcended his lifelong biases and public image. If my father could take such a bold step to let go of his internal and societal doctrines, then I knew I could as well.

People often ask me what was it that changed my father's mind about my husband. I believe that deep in his heart, my father had a great desire to live beyond the image he had to maintain as one of the most admired public figures in South Korea. He was conflicted in his love for me, and I was confused by a love that seemed so filled with contradictions. On the one hand, he wanted me to be free of the restrictions that he was trapped into, to be happy and to spread my wings. He always told me, "There is no difference between a girl and a boy. Go as far as you can." When you think about it, my father's comment was a revolutionary statement during the 1950s and 1960s in a heavily male-dominated society. On the other hand, my father wanted me to abide by our societal norms and obligations, and follow tradition by marrying a Korean man of our own social standing.

Despite his disapproval of my marriage to a Caucasian, letting me live freely in America was the greatest gift he ever gave me. After my family flew back home from Seoul, my father called unexpectedly. He told me that the most important thing in life was to be happy—a total surprise to hear coming out of his mouth. Regardless of what our culture or our family's reputation dictated, he wanted me to pursue happiness.

Biases are the result of complex emotions, cultural scripts, and personal experiences. My father was caught in the middle of centuries-old cultural values. As a public figure, he had to honor and maintain face by upholding Korean values, expectations, and leading by example. As a father, he wanted his children to be happy. By sympathizing with my father's complicated circumstance and struggles, I overcame my feelings of rejection and started to see past his cultural and public obligations and into his heart. While my experiences with my father are deeply personal, what I learned was universal. By expanding my empathy, I enlarged my capacity to connect—not only with my father, but with anyone who I don't immediately understand or relate to.

Today, while the stigma associated with South Korean women married to Westerners has greatly decreased, interracial marriages are still considered outside the norm and not something that a family would feel outwardly proud of. Even in the United States, interracial marriages were illegal until 1967. We've moved past our old mindset, but it still takes time to loosen our deep-seated values, attitudes, and biases.

Many years after my marriage, I used to be startled whenever I saw an Asian woman with a Caucasian man. I used to hear myself saying, "Oh my, I can't believe she's with a Western man." Automatically, I was thrown back into the judgmental state of my old brain, forgetting for a moment that I was married to a white man. It fascinated me that, subconsciously, I could continue to live with such an overt double standard. After all these years being away from the Korean culture, I am reminded by how long-lasting my embedded cultural beliefs stayed inside of me.

Racial Bias

Similar to my father's prejudice against my husband, my father-in-law had biases against me. It took a few years for me to realize the extent of his antipathy, but I would sense it at random times.

My father-in-law was a proud American of German heritage, and he was not what you would call the warmest of men. Usually found in front of the television watching tennis with a Budweiser and peanuts, he believed in "helping others" and "doing the right thing"—a strong base of Midwestern philosophy that I have always respected. Like my father, he served in the Korean War, but in the Navy, and he carried the notion that South Korea still owed America for US support in the war. He believed that Koreans should be more grateful to America for fighting and protecting them from the communists.

When he found out that my father did not accept his son as a son-in-law for being an American, he was furious. In fact, before our wedding, Steve and I had to make up a white lie about the reason why my parents were not able to attend. Ten days prior to our wedding, a Korean Air Lines flight en route to Seoul from New York was shot down by the Soviet Union. The plane crashed into the Sea of Japan, killing all 269 passengers and crew members. Although this tragic incident resulted in a tense moment of the Cold War, Steve and I used it as our excuse for why my family couldn't attend, stating that my father was dealing with political turmoil.

During the thirty years that I have known my father-in-law, he has never asked or showed any interest in my culture or my background. Initially, I assumed he was moody or quiet by nature, but over time it became impossible to ignore the warmth and acceptance he showed the Caucasian wives of my husband's brothers. I understood why he would resent my family, especially after the snub of not attending the wedding.

As justified as he was to feel that way, I sensed that his resentment toward me was about something more. However, it never occurred to me that my father-in-law would be prejudiced against me for being Asian. After all, at least outwardly, he was always polite to me throughout the time Steve and I were dating, and at our wedding. Slowly, over time, he became more distant and I truly felt that he did not like me. For example, he never made direct eye contact. He never included me in conversations. He always directed questions about our children exclusively to Steve. While I was in the same room with him, I may as well have not existed.

Years later when our daughter, Sophia, was six and our son, Michael, was four, my in-laws came to visit our home in Washington, DC. On a warm summer evening, the four of us decided to go for a walk through the neighborhood. Our home was located in a beautiful section of the city near Georgetown, where many foreign diplomats lived. As we waited for my mother-in-law, the three of us stood outside, chatting by the street.

A well-dressed young Asian couple in their early thirties strolled down the sidewalk. For all we knew, they could have been diplomats or new neighbors. Without any warning, my father-in-law said, "What are they doing here?" implying that Asians shouldn't be allowed to live in such a nice area. I was shocked, unable to believe the words that just came out of his mouth. Steve was furious and mortified. Luckily, the young couple was out of earshot, but I was devastated. My father-in-law was visiting our home to see his two half-Asian grandchildren, and he was still completely oblivious to his own racial prejudice. I hadn't seen it coming.

Looking back, I believe either my father-in-law temporarily forgot his Korean daughter-in-law was standing next to him or that his deep-rooted bias came out of him subconsciously without a second thought. After the incident, the three of us never spoke of it again or asked what he really meant by his comment. My husband didn't have an open relationship with his father where he could speak honestly about anything. Similar to the way I was around my father, Steve had to watch what he said around his father. However, my husband and I were both disappointed by this comment and seeing this side of him.

Our fathers, both gone now, couldn't have been more different in terms of appearance, background, or culture. Yet, they were similar in so many ways. Both stressed the importance of their family's public image and lived with deep-seated values that turned into behaviors of bias and prejudice. Sadly, they lost the most precious thing they had: connection with family. While our fathers' prejudice stemmed from different places, my father coming from his cultural upbringing and Steve's father from ingrained racial bias, both derive from the same domain of closed-mindedness.

Face and Reason

Face and reason are two of the most powerful forces that dictate people's behaviors and actions. In Eastern cultures, face governs everything about a person: personal and family reputation, self-worth, prestige, and respect. Losing face feels like life and death, while gaining face feels almost spiritual in the sense that it lifts one's entire being. As you can imagine, people will do anything to protect their face and the face of their family with the utmost vigilance.

To Westerners, "face" may best be compared to image or reputation. This is only a literal translation. While Westerners may relate to embarrassment or shame, it's hard to fully grasp the depth in which face affects a person's whole being. This gap in understanding stems from the core philosophical differences between cultures.

Having a sense of independence and individualism is an essential part of the Western ethos. Look no further than US history to see examples of independence and the Wild West mentality. Individualism is ingrained from an early age and reinforced throughout one's life in the West. In contrast to the West, Eastern culture is shaped by collective group mentality. One's personal identity is directly integrated with the collective mindset of one's family, team, group, and country. Through the cultural collective mentality, at the cost of individualism, there is a pervasive sense of connection that is felt beneath all interactions, including nonverbal communication. As an illustrative example, in Asia, one's family name is written first. For example, John Smith would be addressed and written as Smith John. This naming convention portrays how one carries his or her identity, placing emphasis on family over self.

In the East, promoting oneself would be viewed as offensive and selfish. Imagine the idea of face in terms of layers—like the layers of an onion. On the outside, Easterners reflect the collective face of one's own country—Korea, Japan, China, etc. Under those layers are smaller layers devoted toward one's family or work. Deep inside, the smallest layers reflect the self, which are often not seen. When I was growing up, my father always put his time and focus into the country over his family. He was absent during most of my childhood and teenage years, and missed out on family vacations, school functions, and even my high school graduation. After my children started elementary school in Washington, DC, I was shocked to find recognizable senators and politicians attending the same school functions that I did. I thought, "Shouldn't they be working right now? It's wonderful that they put family before country."

An individual can lose face for him- or herself, for family, for the group, or for the country. While it may seem like an extreme example, harakiri or seppuku, a Japanese form of ritual suicide, served as an honorable alternative to disgrace. Harakiri epitomizes the power of face and self-shame as it takes the responsibility for losing the face of the self, the family, and the country. It involved cutting the belly open with a sword, turning the blade, and pulling it out, ensuring death with honor. Harakiri can be traced back to the era of Samurai from 1185 to 1868, and as recently as World War II. As far as I know, I don't believe any Americans committed harakiri or suicide after losing a battle.

While the concept of face may govern the East, reason and logic reign in the West. From my experience in the West, unless something is proven, it doesn't count. We can't prove that there is a destiny. We can't prove that all ailments have roots in the mind-body-spirit connection. We can't prove that *Chi/Ki*—an Eastern term meaning life-source, which has no Western translation—controls our well-being.

Western philosophy is very much driven by logic, linearism, facts, and results. In general, feelings are relegated to the back seat. After my US corporate career in global marketing, I became an executive leadership coach to help increase clients' leadership capacity and relational management. When coaching Western clients, more often than not I had to convince them that emotions, not intellect, drive our behaviors and actions. When my clients finally confronted and explored their feelings, that's when they started making real progress.

Both face and reason can get in the way of living full and free lives. We can see the differences between East and West, between my father and father-in-law, and how group mentality and individualism split culturally. While the cultures of East and West may seem distinct from each other, the bridge between the two is getting shorter.

In recent years, the East has adapted more of a Western mindset. Fifteen years ago, I plunged into therapy, coaching, and leadership development workshops that challenged and pushed me to explore painful truths about myself and the impact of my early scripts. I'll never forget breaking down in front of an entire workshop, flushing out repressed feelings that I held for a lifetime. It was cathartic and healing in ways I never experienced before. In the East, this kind of endeavor would be viewed as a selfish act and disrespectful to your upbringing; you are supposed to accept your destiny as it was given to you. Not only would I have been restricted by worries about saving face, but I would have been viewed as someone who was not emotionally stable. People would have thought something was seriously wrong with me and my family for pursuing therapy and self-development work. Fortunately, times are changing.

Around 2014, I visited Seoul and had a chance to speak with one of my middle-school classmates who has since become a psychiatrist. I was very impressed by the courageous career choice she made more than thirty years ago and the way psychiatry is now being accepted in South Korea. In the past, an individual who had mental health problems was viewed as defective—a social outcast. In addition, the stability of the entire family's mental health would be questioned. It would be assumed that the individual's family must have a defective gene pool—damaging the face of the entire family. While the situation has improved, the acceptance of psychiatry is not as widespread as it is in America. However, the perception has changed tremendously from what I remember. In Korea, the department of psychiatry used to be called mental disease, but it has since changed to mental health.

As the East has slowly adapted Western philosophies, so has the West adapted Eastern philosophies. The idea behind holistic health, the nature of mind-body-sprit connection, originates from the East. Acupuncture, Chinese herbal medicine, yoga, meditation, and visualization all originated in Asia centuries ago. You wouldn't know that today! Think about how often you see people carrying their yoga mats down the street. Holistic and spiritual work is becoming far more commonplace and widely practiced in America.

For a long time, Western medicine widely dismissed alternative medicine from the East. Similarly, my maternal grandfather, a doctor who was trained in Western medicine, held back from using Western treatments, such as drugs and surgery, in favor of holistic treatments. He believed that our body and mind together had the power to heal and revitalize our life energy. It is ironic how Eastern medicine embraced holistic health yet dismissed psychotherapy. In our globalized world, we are now learning from each other, melding our differences, and expanding our horizons.

The Universal Language

People frequently ask me, "What language do you dream in?" It's a question I cannot answer definitively. It may seem logical that my primary language is the one I'd most likely dream in. However, I switched my primary language from Korean, my native tongue and the first language I ever acquired, to English, which I have been speaking for more than fifty years. At this point, my English is better than my Korean.

Once we start learning new languages, the way we think and see the world starts to shift as well. The idea that thoughts and language are intertwined can be understood through the Sapir-Whorf Linguistic Relativity hypothesis. It proposes that the language one speaks reflects and shapes the way one thinks and behaves in a particular culture and that people from different languages and cultures may see the world differently due to linguistic differences.[1] I experienced firsthand the intimately interwoven relationship between language, culture, and way of thinking, having gone through the process of learning other tongues.

So what language do I dream in? According to my husband, in my dreams, I speak in both English and Korean. Honestly, I don't know. Sometimes, I remember a few words, but it's blurred if they were in Korean or English. I have thought long and hard, trying to figure this out. Is this because I forget dreams the moment I wake up? No. I recall my dreams often and even quite vividly.

The truth is that I do not recall the language from my dreams, but rather thoughts, images, and feelings. In dreams, language rarely plays a factor; what does matter is the way I feel, for that is what I remember most: fear, excitement, anxiety, sadness, joy, or countless other emotions are what I take away, not words. The same can be said for memories and previous life experience. Think about it. Recall your favorite childhood memory or event, perhaps listening to a great speaker or learning from your favorite teacher. From that memory, do you recall the words that were spoken verbatim or do you recall the emotion and wisdom in which those words were expressed and the way that person made you feel? My guess is that it's the latter.

While the Sapir-Whorf hypothesis may help explain the differences between cultures and people that are influenced by the spoken language, the link between language and thought are complicated and nebulous.[2] Despite this inherent complexity, I believe there is one universal language—a form of communication that transcends languages and cultures. By no means am I an expert or linguistic authority; nonetheless, I believe that our thoughts and feelings can be conveyed and shared universally, no matter what culture one is from or with whom they interact. While I certainly remember words and phrases, I don't define my personal encounters through words but rather through our shared feelings and connections. Think about the feelings you may get from the loving hugs of your parents, loved ones, or close friends; exchanged smiles with strangers; or the emotions provoked from beautiful music or a sad movie. The list is abundant. We all speak the universal language, the connecting glue that spreads widely under all varied and distinct languages around the world.

Essential Takeaways

- Diverse cultural upbringings shape diverse mindsets and ways of life. Despite our distinctions, we aren't different beings. While we may diverge in many ways, we can always connect through our humanity. This effortless flow creates openness and comfort in navigating through mixed cultural environments.
- By embracing cultural differences and human similarities, we deepen our empathy and understanding of others. Through our effort, we accumulate knowledge and flexibility to adopt, tolerate, or reject what we assimilate, thus enriching our lives beyond our boundaries.

7

CROSS-CULTURAL AGILITY

Expanding Relational Aptitude

Have you ever had an encounter with someone who didn't speak your language, yet the two of you instantly felt a nonverbal connection? Perhaps a smile revealed openness without an agenda or a hidden bias. This beautiful human essence is inside all of us. This is the driving force behind connection despite differences. I still remember with deep warmth my immediate connection with that black boy sixty years ago. It was a beautiful encounter of human essences between two children that transcended language, skin color, and cultural barriers.

The desire to belong and identify with others is an inherent part of our existence. Naturally, we feel more comfortable with those who appear similar to us rather than with those who seem different. This may explain why people are so deeply connected to their race, why we cheer for our own countries during the Olympics, or why we sympathize with people who have similar ethnic backgrounds more so than others.

As the saying goes, birds of a feather flock together. Even for those whose families have lived in another country for three or more generations, many have an emotional loyalty and attachment to their origins. Beyond ethnic origins, people feel connections more quickly with others who have shared bonds in socioeconomics, alumni groups, social clubs, professional associations, religious beliefs, etc. There is a vertical and horizontal similarity among all people—vertical refers to physical boundaries such as culture and race; horizontal refers to lifestyle and career—that cuts across cultures and ethnicity.

If we can learn to find commonalities within our differences, we can expand our connections and build stronger relationships. No matter who you interact with, there are three key elements that define each of us: our common human essence, individuality, and cultural differences. By seeing that each of us is a blend of these three components, we can expand our outlook toward cultural and human differences.

The Power of Human Connection

Cross-cultural agility is about one's relational capacity to connect with others while navigating through differences. Although cultures may be quite distinct from one another, there are no profound differences about being human; we each share the universal bond of common human essence—hope, love, happiness, acceptance, sadness, fear, anger, spirituality, and ambition are traits that every single human possesses.

Seeing an individual beyond cultural differences immediately opens the human space to connect. Through our body language and nonverbal communication, we emit our intentions and attitudes. When I feel that a person is being genuine and warm, I open up naturally and create a circle of kinship, even if a single word has not been spoken.

When you interact with another person, regardless of where he or she may be from, what language they speak, or the color of their skin, you are first and foremost interacting with another human being who shares the same universal human bonds that you do. By connecting through the common human essence, we create a comfortable and connected space that narrows the gap between our differences. With some people, I immediately feel at ease despite our physical and cultural differences. With others, I feel self-conscious and distant no matter how similar we may be. The openness every person brings with them is what makes the difference. It's a two-way street: I have to do my part, and they have to do theirs. As I started to open up more, I expanded the channel for mutual connection.

Although it is possible for any one of us to create meaningful connections with others, cross-cultural agility isn't easy for everyone. While we may assume that cross-cultural agility is the exclusive domain of people who have been exposed to diverse cultures early on, what truly matters is the innate ability to connect with others, a genuine quality that no amount of traveling or exposure to other cultures can make up for. I've encountered many people who don't feel confident about interacting with other cultures because of their lack of experience. Many of these people grew up in small towns and rarely interacted with other cultures. Surprisingly, I find that some of these people are even more cross-culturally agile than those who have lived, worked, or traveled around the world.

Barriers of Navigating a New World

Do you remember how you felt on your first day of high school or when you started a new job? Nervous? Excited? Scared? When we branch out of our comfort zone, feeling out of place is only natural. It's easy to see why the idea of interacting with a foreign culture can be intimidating.

To me, and to many other foreigners, language is the most apparent inadequacy that causes feelings of self-doubt and reduces confidence. Even after fifty years of speaking English, I am still self-conscious about my accent and my speaking and writing abilities. For foreigners, speaking to others in English, or in any other language besides their mother tongue, is very intimidating. When I came to the United States for college after four years of high school in Mexico City, my English was still quite shaky. I gravitated to science, not because I had a proclivity for it but because it didn't require as much English as other subjects. Language barriers may be a reason why we see many foreigners in science and math.

After college and two years of graduate school in science, I decided to move out of that field. With the ambition to build a successful corporate career, I plunged into business school. As a mandate to graduate, my business school required in-class verbal participation, which was my biggest nightmare. Not only was I worried about participating and making solid points in class, I was even more concerned that I sounded like an idiot who could barely speak English. While I was so nervous about sounding eloquent and articulate, I forgot the whole reason why I was speaking to begin with.

You can imagine the terror I experienced every time I raised my hand. It was a lose-lose situation. If I didn't speak, I would fail the class. When I did speak, I felt like an inarticulate fool. I became paralyzed with fear. When I spoke in class, I was always thinking to myself, No one can understand anything I'm saying. To me, the other students spoke so articulately and effortlessly that they only compounded my feelings of inadequacy, regardless of the substance of their remarks.

To my surprise, I found out that most of my classmates were just as terrified of speaking as I was. While they were worried about making impactful comments, I was worried only about sounding good. In fact, several of my friends failed classes and were kicked out of school because they hardly spoke up, even though they had the advantage of speaking English their whole lives. Once I discovered everyone was just as frightened as I was, albeit for different reasons, I felt a little more confident. At least now we were all in the same boat of anxiety and I was no longer floating adrift on my own.

One day, after speaking up nervously and stumbling on my words, there was a long silence. After a moment, my professor turned to everyone and said, "Did anyone understand a word she just said?" It felt like a punch to the gut. I could feel the air being sucked out of my stomach as I sank back in my chair. I was so hurt and humiliated, even though I knew instinctively that his intention wasn't to put me down. My professor's aim was to teach us to get to the point sooner, be clear, and be succinct.

What he saw was my hesitancy, my lack of the ability to articulate clearly and confidently. Regardless of what I understood his intentions to be, I could not speak up in any of my classes afterward.

My anxiety mounted, knowing that if I didn't speak up in class, I would fail out of school, and that was not an option for me. I knew I had to have a conversation with my professor in person. As terrified as I was, I requested a meeting. To my surprise, the professor could not have been more supportive and apologetic. He had no idea how I felt or the damage that one comment had inflicted on me. During our meeting, I requested that he call on me in class, which would force me to speak. Although I never got over the anxiety of speaking out loud in class, I was becoming more comfortable with myself, the first step toward feeling agile in a foreign world.

Through our openness to explore our differences and understand each other, my professor and I broadened our understanding of one another. He never understood my perspective before our meeting, and I helped open his eyes to how language plays a major role in insecurity. He helped me focus on the content of my speech rather than the sound of it. This powerful lesson changed the way I looked at language and convinced me that the substance of one's speech matters more than how it is spoken.

Misleading Assumptions

Several years ago, my friend Bill, a real-estate developer, led a team that purchased a major Washington, DC, landmark office building. A proud American, Bill is an open and direct guy. At the time, Bill was working with a large Japanese bank as his financial partner, and every two weeks, the Japanese executives would fly in from Tokyo to meet and discuss the progress of the construction and leasing.

At the end of each meeting, Bill asked the Japanese executives whether they were pleased with the progress. Each time, they responded that they were very pleased. Several months later, to Bill's shock, a team of auditors, outside engineers, and leasing consultants showed up and took over the process without a word of warning. It turned out that the Japanese executives were actually unhappy with Bill's work, even though they had been telling him the exact opposite. Bill and his team were angry and dispirited at being forced to work under a new team without any previous discussion. This resentment created a toxic environment, and soon cooperation broke down between all parties. Construction issues arose that were not resolved, leasing slowed down, and approximately $25 million to $50 million of value was lost.

Bill's issues with the Japanese echo similar sentiments I often hear from many of my Western friends and colleagues: Ambiguous communication is one of the biggest challenges when dealing with Asian business partners. In Asia, "yes" doesn't necessarily mean yes; rather, it often means "no" or "maybe" or "I don't know." You might be wondering: how am I supposed to do business with anyone from Asia? This must be quite frustrating, particularly for business executives from America where, most of the time, one's desires and intentions are clearly articulated.

In Asia, building personal relationships comes before business. Whenever two new business partners meet, there is a feeling-out process that is often overlooked in the West. In America, we like things fast and to the point. In Asia, cutting to the chase so quickly is considered impolite and aggressive.

Knowing my friend Bill as I do, and looking at the situation from the perspective of the Japanese executives, I can conjecture that they may have been uncomfortable with his direct and aggressive approach and felt resentment. Or maybe the Japanese executives were uncomfortable saying "I don't know" because of fear of embarrassment or losing face. Saying "no" could have suggested that they were lacking humility and respect for others, which are expected virtues. It's also possible that the Japanese executives felt that Bill's friendly and informal style wasn't deferential enough to the senior executives. Unfortunately, there are no simple answers when dealing with cultural complexities and seeming contradictions.

Clashes are inevitable in our lives, especially when they are rooted in cultural differences. Clearly, Bill and the Japanese executives didn't develop a shared understanding. Regardless, Bill inadvertently failed to create a connecting channel through which the Japanese could feel at ease enough to ask questions. At the same time, the Japanese executives were accountable for not sharing their point of view. However, neither was at fault. They were each operating under the mutual desire to produce successful results.

If Bill was more knowledgeable and attuned to Japanese culture, could it have made a difference? Maybe. Maybe not. Bill learned a lot from this failed venture, and he gained a better respect for the difficulties of building successful relationships across cultures. He realized that he can't make assumptions about business partners from other parts of the world and presume they operate the same way he does. It takes time, patience, and respect to understand others and build relationships. Cultural knowledge, empathy, humility, and trust are the ingredients vital to garnering a shared understanding.

Pigeonholing

During my business career, it was always assumed that I was an expert on Asian and South Korean markets. In reality, I have always worked in the United States. Regardless of my qualifications or résumé, I was always a recommended candidate for relocation in Asia, even though I was not an expert on the region. I couldn't help but feel as though I was being reduced to a cultural stereotype and not seen for my accomplishments.

As a South Korean woman, I was automatically labeled as someone who would be a better fit in the South Korean or Asian markets. I was being viewed through a culturally biased and pigeonholed lens, not seen for my own merit or previous experience, but rather my culture. Of course, my deep Asian heritage is always a part of me, but cultural knowledge is only one element that defines one's potential for success. In fact, I knew numerous people, both from the East and the West, who were far more qualified for the position than I was.

Business skills are individual attributes that transcend culture and race. The only advantage I had was my Asian upbringing. Many of my international colleagues experienced the same frustrations and felt they were being stereotyped into their own culture or country of origin.

Pigeonholing impacts an organization's effectiveness. To be a powerful global engine, an organization must behave as a seamless unit with a strong sense of camaraderie and openness in the pursuit of collective goals. This open energy is the glue that sustains pervasive diversity and bolsters competitiveness. Instead, what I frequently experienced was a global entity made up of loose parts without a cohesive core.

Defining and differentiating cultures can be a double-edged sword. On one hand, there are clear distinctions we must be aware of. On the other hand, it would be distancing to apply those characteristics to every person within a particular culture. Wouldn't it be unfair for a foreigner to assume that all Americans love cheeseburgers and milkshakes or that every Irishman loves to drink? When you think about it, there really is no such thing as a typical American, Chinese, Mexican, British, Indian, Korean, French, Japanese, and so on. Rather, we are each unique individuals with our own strengths and weaknesses that transcend race and culture.

Trying Too Hard

It's in our nature to want to fit in and please others. This innate human desire makes people try far too hard to fit in to try and gain the approval of others. Whether it's starting a new job, trying to network at a social, or making friends in school or work, regardless of culture, all humans go through the same experience of trying to fit in.

Meeting new people is challenging enough, but when we meet people from a different culture, things can get even more difficult. Many of us frequently become hypersensitive or overly accommodating, to the point of being inauthentic. While well intended, this overcompensation can lead to affectations that create distance, discomfort, and other unintended outcomes that keep people at arm's length. Regardless of cultural differences, this is a universal behavior that we can all relate to at one point or another. Newcomers who enter into a different culture and natives who interact with outsiders can both feel unsure about how to interact with one another. Throughout my life, I have been guilty of this behavior, whether it was when I was first starting school in Seoul, attending The American School in Mexico, or assimilating into America.

In regards to my insecurities about English, I initially thought that if I could perfect English, I wouldn't feel as different. I had an illogical fear that my accent was holding me back from making new friends and connections. I remember how my excessive effort to attain perfect English backfired.

During a speaking presentation in front of more than sixty people, I went completely blank when it was my turn. My brain froze. The night before, I stayed up all night, memorizing my speech, agonizing over every word and small mistake I might make. On stage, I spoke robotically, focusing only on my mistakes and not connecting with my audience. Even though I barely got through my speech, I learned a valuable lesson: I'd rather speak genuinely through broken English than to speak perfectly but not be myself. Would you rather speak to someone who uses their full heart with incorrect grammar or someone who attempts to speak perfectly but who is not present?

Trying too hard is a two-way street. While I've certainly done my fair share, I've also been on the receiving end. For example, oftentimes when new acquaintances learn that I am Korean, they jump to the conclusion that I know everything about Korea and therefore dictate the topic of conversation to only Korea. Just because I am Korean doesn't mean that I know everything about Korea and only want to talk about Korea. I left that country fifty years ago! It would be like saying all Americans are George Washington experts just because he was America's first president.

When people have conversations with me exclusively about South Korea or Asian culture, it's hard to feel included or embraced. While well intended, these gestures can often end up undermining relationships. My issue is not with their questions or gestures, it's with being viewed and treated as a Korean first and foremost, not as Soo. These people may be genuinely interested about getting to know me but assume that conversing on culture is the best way to build connection.

There are so many other ways to connect beyond culture. It would be better to ask questions about where I grew up, where I want to visit next, whether I have children, what my children do, my likes, my dislikes, etc. There is so much more to a person than just their culture. I'm not suggesting that culture cannot be discussed, but to also consider all the other ways you can make genuine connections that build strong relationships. Would you rather be the first person to ask a foreigner about their favorite movie or the 217th to ask about their culture? Once we make genuine human connections, any topic will become open and not viewed as stereotypical.

My brother, a successful international businessman, would constantly complain about his many trips to the United States because of the same reason: His American business partners always took him out to Asian restaurants. Living in Korea, my brother ate Asian food almost every day and always looked forward to his trips to America so he could get a great steak. Unfortunately, my brother's business partners tried to accommodate his cultural background more than his specific preferences.

By trying to make my brother feel at home, they made him feel like a cultural stereotype. After this happened repeatedly, my brother started suggesting dinner options when he came to visit. I often see people being overly sensitive toward foreigners the way my brother's business partners were to my brother. In extreme cases, it feels as though we are treating foreigners like people with special needs. Some people end up being so over-the-top in their gestures of accommodation and attempts at connection that it all comes off as artificial. When we place culture before people, that's when we lose human connections.

Being Yourself

When we meet a new friend or neighbor, we usually don't overthink how we should act; it's second nature. So why do we act so differently when we meet someone from a foreign culture? When people feel intimidated by differences, often they behave uncharacteristically from their normal self in an attempt to create a sense of comfort. I've seen many contrived affectations that can come across as inauthentic or off-putting. People who laugh at unfunny jokes, smile way too big, or constantly bring up cultural questions as a way to bridge differences. This contrived behavior can create the opposite intended effect, and it causes distance and division.

Being at ease with unfamiliarity is not as much about gaining knowledge about what you don't know or acting in a way that you think is appropriate, as it is about being comfortable with yourself.

It's natural that we would want to be respectful of differences in others. However, when we are too focused on how we should act, we may forgo our authenticity. Cross-cultural agility requires you to be you: the simplest yet most difficult behavior. People connect through humanity, not cultural etiquettes or preconceived ideas of appropriateness. Although human connection transcends cultural gaps, I wouldn't be honest if I didn't say it takes time to feel comfortable in an entirely different environment or with people from another culture. I thought by acting like someone else, I would feel more comfortable and accepted by others. In reality, we can't change who we are overnight, nor should we try to. I learned that to feel at ease in a new environment, I couldn't pretend to be someone else. I had to be comfortable with who I was.

No one should expect a foreigner to know about other cultures in-depth. When you run into uncertainties, ask the person you're speaking to for guidance. If you approach them with openness, honesty, and without apology, you won't go wrong. You might say, "I am not quite sure what would be the most appropriate manner," "I would like to avoid coming across as insensitive or disrespectful," or "I would appreciate your ongoing help and advice."

As simple as these words may sound, it takes courage to express them, and you will be pleasantly surprised by the powerful effect of this simple and genuine gesture. In these situations, many people often fail to speak up and simply nod their heads without understanding what just transpired. In reality, when you politely ask for clarification or admit you didn't understand what was said, you will gain respect for speaking honestly, which will draw people in. In time, your authenticity will produce rewards. Not only will it spare you the mental exhaustion of trying too hard, you will also gain knowledge and build connecting relationships, all the while being at ease with yourself. Remember, no one can know everything.

Knowledge vs. Embodiment

In today's multicultural world, business is becoming increasingly competitive. Companies like to value professionals who possess a global mindset, but what does that really mean? Is global mindset something that we can learn or master? Does it mean we must first obtain an in-depth understanding of every single country and culture in the world? Is that even possible?

The truth is that a global mindset encompasses much more than global knowledge and experience—it describes one's frame of mind. Without question, cultural knowledge is a valuable asset when trying to better understand people from another culture. Additionally, cultural experience deepens cultural knowledge. But just because you have obtained knowledge doesn't mean you possess a global mindset.

I have worked with global executives who traveled, lived in, and conducted business all over the world. Two such executives I encountered, John and Patricia, approached their business dealings with different attitudes. On paper, both were extremely accomplished and well-versed in the worldwide market, but John had a significant advantage in terms of achievements and experience.

Early on, John was exposed to various cultures in Asia and Europe, having had a father with a successful military career in the US Air Force. John had an impeccable educational background, attending elementary and high school overseas, and college and business school in the United States. For more than twenty years, John built a successful career in finance, both in the United States and overseas. He is what many would describe as having a strong global mindset. Yet, despite his early exposure to diverse cultures, his competencies, and extensive global business experience, John could be arrogant and close-minded. He had a difficult time connecting with people beyond the surface level. Many people felt he was rigid, unable to fully listen to the opinions of others or acknowledge his shortcomings.

On the other hand, Patricia didn't live overseas and hadn't been exposed to other cultures until her international business trips. Even though her educational background was on par with John's, she only had twelve years of business experience compared to John's twenty years, and only five years in global business. However, what Patricia did have was a capacity to connect with and motivate those around her by being humble and open-minded. Her perspective and attitude transcended borders, cultures, and races, and created a pervasive feeling of connection.

What limited John from maximizing his success wasn't his cultural knowledge or experience; it was his mindset and attitude. What Patricia lacked in experience and cultural knowledge, she made up for in humanity and openness. People flocked to her and loved being in her company. Ultimately, Patricia became far more successful.

As we can see from this example, while John possessed abundant cultural knowledge and global experience, he didn't possess an open mind. It's not about the knowledge; it's about how one uses it. *Global mindset* is a mindset, not an academic term. A mindset is a part of our being—how we think, feel, and act—and how we intrinsically connect with others. No amount of traveling or exposure can make up for a lack of human connection.

Bridging Forces

A former colleague of mine, an American businesswoman I will call Barbara, inadvertently caused her Asian client to lose face. In a critical business meeting, she rejected one of the suggestions her client made in front of everyone by pointing out his company's previous failures. In America, her assertiveness and strategic argument would have helped to build her credibility; however, in this situation, her comments caused her Asian client to feel ashamed. He went silent after Barbara's comment, and she quickly realized she had overstepped her boundaries. Even though Barbara was aware of the importance of face in Asia, she reverted to her assertive self.

After the meeting, Barbara profusely apologized to her client. She candidly spoke about her difficulties keeping up with cultural protocols when under pressure. Honesty moves people regardless of what culture a person comes from. Throughout the course of her five-year relationship with her client, Barbara established a strong and trusting bond between them. Her client trusted and respected Barbara, and relied heavily on her for strategic guidance and support. Her accidental cultural mishap was smoothed over and the two parties were able to continue their business collaboratively.

This incident also speaks volumes about her client's open-mindedness, empathy, and trust, and his strength to transcend the loss of face. The invisible human bond that Barbara was able to build with her client through the years helped her overcome the cultural mishap. If we can trust the person in front of us and they can trust us, together we can overcome many seemingly insurmountable cultural difficulties and challenges.

Despite all our training, knowledge, and positive intentions, cultural mishaps and misunderstandings are bound to happen. We can't always be cultural chameleons, replicating foreign norms and customs perfectly. This might all sound contradictory and confusing—juggling between being yourself, speaking honestly, not trying too hard, and abiding by cultural differences. It can be a headache, but developing cross-cultural agility is not a linear formula. Knowledge, experience, and building human connections are *all* essential ingredients for cross-cultural agility. Cross-cultural agility is not a formula. If there is one takeaway, it would be: success depends on expanding our relational capacity that is built upon trust and empathy.

Barbara's aggressive and assertive behavior got her to where she was in the United States, but it was not an admirable trait in the East. She knew this very well, but under pressure, it's easy to revert to our familiar behavioral patterns. Making mistakes is part of any relationship. The beauty is that strong bonds can overcome most human errors.

Essential Takeaways

- Cross-cultural agility is a vital attribute that advances personal, business, and political relationships. This agility is foremost built on human qualities—empathy, openness, humility, and confidence—that transcends race, gender, culture, knowledge, and experience.
- Attaining this capacity is built upon one's genuine desire to see and interact with people as an individual, not as a representative of a culture. Authenticity radiates connective energy, the foundation for constructing a connecting space to learn about each other, build invisible human bonds, and accomplish mutually beneficial outcomes.
- Defining an individual by their culture is a simplistic view. Within every culture there exist universal human dynamics—love and hate, freedom and burden, acceptance and discrimination. From this perspective, we can nourish human connection and reduce the distance between our differences.

- Narrow lenses create narrow perspectives and limit personal growth. In workplaces, narrow lenses cost organizational effectiveness and the bottom line. It reduces a company's potential to fully develop and leverage its varied talent pool, and to foster inclusion and cooperation of varied beliefs, backgrounds, and expertise. On the other hand, open lenses drive inclusive perspectives, which drives strategy, and ultimately results.

ADVANCING
PERVASIVE
DIVERSITY

8

UNINTENDED CONSEQUENCES

Calling for Bold Changes

After all of the time, energy, and resources invested into improving diversity and integration—through affirmative action, equal opportunity mandates, and racial quota goals—how can we still be so divided? This question is a somber reminder of how complicated and daunting the task of promoting diversity is. Diversity is not grounded in numbers or formulas; we are dealing with human dynamics that cannot be solved by asserting one particular ideology or implementing by-the-book solutions. There is an enormous contradiction that needs to be addressed in regard to diversity progress.

Labeling and Categorizing

During my first year living in the United States as a freshman in college, I remember meeting a young woman in my chemistry lab. She was quiet, friendly, and always diligent in her work. She was a commuter student, so I didn't see her on campus very often. In the limited time we spent together, we worked well as a team and I liked her very much.

One evening in the dining hall, I mentioned this young woman to my friends. In unison, my friends said, "Oh, her? She's Jewish, didn't you know that?" Being new to America, I didn't know what Jewish was. Judging from the tones and facial expressions of my friends, I thought Jewish must be something awful. I didn't ask my friends what Jewish meant. I didn't want them to think I was stupid for not knowing something that seemed so obvious.

Every time I worked with that young woman in the lab after that conversation, I found myself trying to figure out what it was about her that I wasn't seeing. To me, she looked just as Western as my other American friends. Yet when my friends labeled her as Jewish, an invisible wall was suddenly erected within my mind. The next time I was in the chemistry lab with her, I subconsciously changed the way I saw her and interacted with her. I was more cautious and felt more distant, even though I couldn't see what this Jewish thing was all about.

Without saying a word, the energy between us shifted. I am sure she must have sensed the change in me. Based on the comments of my friends, I altered the human space between us. No longer was I just interacting with another person; now I was seeing her differently because of the label that had been attached to her in my mind. The more attention a person pays to something that is highlighted—whether real or imagined—the more conscious one becomes of it.

I see the experience with my Jewish classmate as a microcosm for the damaging effects of stereotypes and the associations attached with labels. Not knowing better, I bought into a secondhand false reality that directly impacted my perception of who she was. Eventually, I learned that "Jewish" was just another ethnicity and religion. I realized my friends were closed-minded and carried their own biases and prejudices.

As a natural progression of the overarching diversity policies and preferential measures, our society and culture have become conditioned to label people based on their race, ethnicity, or color of skin. Labeling has become such an integral part of our mental construct that it is something we don't even think about.

We are creatures of habit: The more we do it, the more we become it. The more we use racial labels, the more we think of people and perceive people by their race and not as individuals. To summarize an entire person by their race is a grave injustice to that person's individuality. The human being underneath the label disappears not only visibly but mentally. Every time we hear or address a person by a label, we reinforce and intensify our habitual patterns of defining people within a narrow band. Our prevalent usage of racial labeling and overemphasis on racial differences pose a major challenge to diversity progress of inclusiveness. We are turning race into an identity, an individual into a group.

Jennifer Eberhardt, a social psychologist at Stanford, and her colleagues contend that perception of physical characteristics may be influenced by racial category labels and social beliefs. In a 2003 study, "Believing Is Seeing: The Effects of Racial Labels and Implicit Beliefs on

Face Perception,"[1] the study participants saw an image of a racially ambiguous-looking man (a morph between a white man and a black man) attached with a racial label. Later, the participants were asked to identify and draw that man. The study concluded that the participants were unable to distinguish the man from his racial label—a microcosm of the impact of labeling. Eberhardt's study helps demonstrate how racial labels perpetuate racial bias.

I believe that we must actively pursue our public and private efforts in reducing systemic racism if we are to advance our society to where differences can coexist harmoniously. I also believe that any anti-racism movement needs to be careful of not further reinforcing our racial labeling culture—creating division rather than inclusiveness. To promote racial equality, we must evolve beyond labels.

To be clear, there is nothing inherently wrong with racial distinctions or labels, but there is a problem with our prevalent practice. We will always have a need for labels to distinguish people. Without labels, we wouldn't be able to obtain accurate census data, reach out to appropriate target audiences for marketing, or describe characteristics. The problem lies within our conditioned tendency to attach stereotypes to labels and group individuals under the same label. There is nothing wrong with being labeled as "white" except when you are then assumed to be a privileged racist. There is no problem being labeled as "black," but there is a problem when that label assumes you are of a negative stereotype.

Unlike other characteristics—such as tall, short, doe-eyed, funny, quiet, etc.—racial labeling carries more connotations than others. Somehow our labels of distinction have clung onto social stereotypes that are changing the meaning behind every label. Not all black people are the same. Not all white people are the same. And so on and so forth. By prolonging our practice of grouping people into racial categories, we continue our divide, moving us further away from our diversity efforts for inclusion and human equality.

Labeling is a powerful and damaging force that prevents human connection. Instead of focusing on connecting through human similarities, we start to emphasize our differences. We have built a mental framework of blanket labeling and blatant stereotyping that I believe is actually a form of deep-seated bias.

Consider how frequently we generalize people into labels and form an opinion of them before we get to know them. By doing so, labeling reinforces a biased mindset that has been prolonging prejudices, discrimination, and dividedness. Worst of all, by labeling others, we begin to see ourselves as a label as well. The stereotypes and stigmas of each race label suddenly become our own. When we no longer see our race as just a characteristic but rather as an identity, we create divides and barriers that separate us from others who are not within our group. For example, the emphasis on identity politics may be the result of groupthink behavior—a result of our labeling practice.

An effective way we can mitigate the downside of labeling and stereotyping is to recondition our perspectives to start seeing the individual behind the label. There is a big difference between acknowledging the differences of others and thinking through stereotyped labels. Through broadening our lens to become color neutral, we see a person much larger than a defined label, whether that label is Asian, white, Hispanic, black, Muslim, transgendered, homosexual, etc.

There are different trains of thought that people exhibit when meeting new people. One train of thought sees the world through labels and racial identifiers. For example, if this kind of person were to meet me for the first time, they may think, "This is an Asian woman, and her name happens to be Soo." Another train of thought sees past labels and connects to the world through the common human essence. These people will think, "Her name is Soo, and she happens to be Asian." Do you see the difference between these two exchanges? Try this the next time you meet someone new. By simply placing your emphasis on the human rather than on the label, you will feel an immediate difference in the way you connect to others, and they will too. Even more importantly, you will feel different about yourself, not as a label, but as a person. I do not believe we are all biased or prejudiced people; rather, we are conditioned by our systems, cultures, and habits to refer to people that way.

Political Correctness

There was a time when minority races and cultures felt as though they had no voice or place; many still do. Political correctness has changed the landscape of America by advancing the visibility and awareness of unique cultures and people. By becoming more sensitive to the way we label people, the goal was to shift the cultural mindset from discrimination to embracement. Unfortunately, labeling is doing the opposite, instead becoming a counterproductive form of political correctness.

On the surface, political correctness makes us believe that labeling is a positive and progressive gesture. By acknowledging another person's race or ethnicity, we believe we are expanding awareness and respect to that person and their heritage. In reality, political correctness has become synonymous to political carefulness—to not say or do anything that could be construed as derogatory to a specific race. This overly alerted attention is changing the way we build human connections and relations. We've become overly obsessed with proper rhetoric and use of our pronouns in fear of offending people.

To me, the practice of labeling and politically correct rhetoric go hand in hand—both noble in intention but damaging in execution. For example, the term *African-American* wasn't coined until the late 1980s by the Rev. Jesse Jackson. Shortly thereafter, our culture started to become overly cautious about the exact words they used when referring to black people, feeling guilty if they didn't use the correct label. Similarly, new terms for ethnicities, genders, and sexuality started to change as well. Words that were inoffensive a decade ago are suddenly offensive today; it's hard to keep track of or know what to say anymore without offending anyone. For example, *Oriental* is now considered a racial epithet for Asians (something I'll never understand), and *African-American* may not be considered the proper label; it may now simply be *black*.

Politically correct culture encourages labeling and proper rhetoric as a way to empower others. As people adopt this way of thinking, the more they label, the more they think they are doing right without considering our ever-increasing dependency on labeling. At the end of the day, labeling is a superficial construct. Politically correct labels cannot shape self-worth or self-image. A label cannot change who we are on the inside. Regardless of the words people choose to describe me (Oriental, Asian, Korean, immigrant), nothing changes who I am beneath the label. No matter how much rhetoric is changed, no matter how much political correctness is enforced, you are the only person who can decide who you are—not the labels or names people call you.

We may be doing too much when it comes to accommodating everyone's self-image through political correctness, but this approach is an impossible task as no one can change or build a person's self-image other than that person. As the word implies, *self-image* is built by the self. Of course, we need to be sensitive and respectful of others. However, the misguided way we go about labeling is obstructing our ability to build a true sense of individuality.

Through time, political correctness has taken on a life of its own. Our culture has become so politically correct that we are filtering the way we connect, share, and communicate. It carries a progressive totalitarian notion about how people should think, feel, and act. Many feel heroic by standing up to those who may use politically incorrect language. We've gotten to the point at which individuals are offended on *behalf* of minorities who themselves wouldn't be offended by what was said or done. We've become so hysterical as a culture that we are demonizing and attacking one another.

After the death of Carrie Fisher, Steve Martin posted the following tweet: "When I was a young man, Carrie

Fisher was the most beautiful creature I had ever seen. She turned out to be witty and bright as well." That same day, Martin deleted this tweet after he received a massive backlash from the feminist community for objectifying Fisher by calling her a "beautiful creature" and not a "woman." I don't know who I am more disappointed by, the hysterical feminists who demonized a man who said nothing wrong or Martin for caving in to these hysterics and deleting it.

We've gotten to the point where people not only feel hesitant to express their thoughts openly, but stop saying anything all together. In a sense, we have lost our freedom of speech in favor of upholding political correctness. We find ourselves tiptoeing around subjects of diversity or race, worried about saying the wrong thing or making the wrong gesture, in fear of being viewed as racists or, even worse, being mired in legal battles.

I am not saying that people should be able to say whatever horrible things come to their mind. I believe we should still be cognizant of others' thoughts and feelings. Nonetheless, we are treading a fine line between being respectful and hypersensitive, between being a normal fallible human being and acting like a politically correct robot. In this atmosphere, it's almost impossible to foster a genuine, comfortable, and connected space between people.

President Donald Trump's victory on November 8, 2016, to become the forty-fifth president of the United States rocked the country with the most unexpected and unprepared outcome. During probably the most divisive and ugly presidential campaign in the country's recent memory, many people felt unable to voice their support for Trump. To be an outspoken Trump supporter was deemed politically incorrect. The outcome was regarded by pollsters, political analysts, and reports to be one of the biggest political upsets in US history.

After the Twitter attack on Steve Martin (post-election), many pointed out that it was this kind of hysterical behavior that may have contributed to Trump's victory. There was a strong undercurrent of anger and resentment against politically correct culture that had gone undetected—because it was not politically correct. In many ways, a vote for Trump was a vote against political correctness.

Even for the progressive left, there is no margin for error when it comes to political correctness. During her 2016 presidential campaign, Hillary Clinton made the following remark: "I have a lot of experience dealing with men who sometimes get off the reservation in the way they behave and how they speak." Her statement brought about a media uproar and was painted as a racially insensitive remark against Native Americans. I sincerely doubt Clinton had any intention of disparaging Native Americans.

While the term "off the reservation" may be offensive to some Native Americans, it's a common phrase, which many people use without considering the context of its original meaning. How far should we go in accusing people without considering human error and unintentional mistakes? We are becoming a culture of finger-pointing and dissecting blemishes that is instigating groupthink behavior.

I am reminded of the deep-seated, guarded concerns many express when I share the main theme of this book: how to bridge the gulf of differences and live beyond labels in diversity. The comments I've received from various people from diverse backgrounds are invariably the same: "That's great; your book is so timely and we need to talk about it." Yet what concerns me is that I also often hear, "I am so happy you are talking about it. You can write about it, but I could not because I am white."

It's alarming and wrong when a group of participants in a society cannot voice what and how they feel. Anyone should be able to write this book or publicly share their thoughts on these subjects, but most feel they cannot. Why should I be exempted? Is it because I am an Asian minority and therefore have a lower possibility of being attacked by social activist groups? Perhaps. I am saddened by the way that so many feel they have to censor or limit themselves in the name of political correctness. That's not political correctness; it's oppression. Most damaging of all, political correctness suppresses a comfortable diversity climate.

When Pop Culture Becomes Political Culture

What happens in the film and television industry often directly reflects our country's political landscape. Just like our country, one of the most controversial issues facing the film industry is racial diversity. I'm not just talking about what we see onscreen, but everything that happens behind the scenes. Before social media, if you didn't like what you watched, you could share your opinion only with a small circle of friends or write a letter to a studio that would never be read. Today, social media has given a voice to people that never had it before. Eventually, when certain points of view become popular or start trending, they can directly impact Hollywood.

Take for example the #OscarsSoWhite social media movement during the 2016 Academy Awards. Demonstrating the power of social media, an activist was credited with starting the hashtag #OscarsSoWhite phenomenon when she tweeted: "It's actually worse than last year. Best Documentary and Best Original Screenplay. That's it. #OscarsSoWhite" Shortly thereafter, others started adopting the #OscarsSoWhite hashtag, and in a matter of hours it was trending worldwide. Never has there been such an outcry over the lack of diversity among the nominees for the Academy Awards, particularly for best actor and actress.

While the lack of diversity in Hollywood might be a justifiable issue, we also need to objectively consider the other side. Who is to say those nominees weren't the very best, regardless of race? The Academy of Motion Picture Arts and Sciences consists of seventeen branches and more than 6,000 voting members. The Actors branch is the largest and is made up of about 1,200 voting members of all colors and races, not twenty white men sitting in a room. Yet, it was nearly impossible to speak out in defense of the Academy's decision to nominate all white actors.

One of the nominees for Best Actress spoke out stating: "Why should we classify people? One can never really know, but perhaps the black actors did not deserve to make the final list [this year] . . . [the #OscarsSoWhite campaign is] racist to white people." Her statements made front-page news and she was lambasted all over social media, painted as an insensitive, privileged, white racist.

The actress's message was that the Oscars should be about the merit of the art, not race and color. Nonetheless, she was berated as an insensitive racist by social media critics and the entertainment press. In a follow-up comment, she stated that: "I regret that my comments could have been misinterpreted this week in my interview with Europe 1 Radio. I simply meant to say that in an ideal world every performance will be given equal opportunities for consideration. I am very honored to be included in this year's wonderful group of nominated actors and actresses."

Things are rarely as clear as black and white, and healthy dialogues and debates are critical, such as whether the 2016 Oscars was an example of systemic racism or purely merit driven. When either side is slammed for voicing an opinion, we are no longer participating in productive engagements. If we can speak to one another honestly and sincerely without fear of judgment or attack, we can then find shared solutions.

As our country has become entrenched with identity politics and political correctness, so has the film industry. Having a son who works in film, I am often surprised by the stories and forced measures that can impact art and creativity. For example, the Screen Actors Guild-American Federation of Television and Radio Artists (SAG-AFTRA) offers film productions a monetary incentive for reaching a specific racial quota in their films. SAG-AFTRA is an American labor union composed of 16,000 actors, performers, and artists worldwide.

If you've ever seen an American film in a movie theater, SAG-AFTRA was most likely responsible for representing all the talent in that film. For example, to receive the incentive for the moderate low to the low budget projects, the production must comply with the following written criteria stipulated on the SAG-AFTRA website:

- A minimum of 50 percent of the total speaking roles and 50 percent of the total days of employment are cast with performers who are members of the following four (4) protected groups: Women, Seniors, Performers with disabilities, and People of color (Black/African American, Asian/Pacific Islander and South Asian, Latino/Hispanic, Arab/Middle Eastern, and Native American)
- A minimum of 20 percent of the total days of employment is cast with performers who are people of color.

On one hand, it's great that SAG-AFTRA is providing more opportunities and incentives for spreading diversity. On the other hand, it can be argued that we are oppressing the freedom of an artist. A producer my son worked with had to recast his film to save money through this incentive. The director had a great actor he wanted to use, but he was forced to replace him. While the production saved money, the director was ultimately unhappy by the casting switch and the performance he received. Is this true diversity?

Word Usage Ramifications

Our progressive culture has become hypervigilant to any hint of actions that may be perceived as discriminatory. While there are justifiable cases of blatant racism and outright discrimination, the pendulum shift of our current racial and political climate has swung to an equally destructive point on the other side.

We see so many cases of irresponsible usage of the words *racist, sexist,* or *bigot* being thrown at people who may not be racist, sexist, or bigoted, but rather just share a different point of view. In their impassioned pursuit, some people can often overstep their boundaries, creating false accusations when others simply disagree or do not join their causes. Under the slogan of political correctness, we witness many people who feel they can get away with saying anything as long it fits the moral template of a politically correct America.

It's easy to get caught up in personal agendas and passions, to let our emotions blind us to rationality, negating original intentions. It's not just one side versus the other—it's our entire social media culture that has created a toxic online environment that seems to be spreading into the real world. If you spend more than five minutes searching under the comment sections on YouTube, Twitter, or Facebook, I'm sure you'll find some incredibly demeaning, crude, and insulting posts by people on both sides of the spectrum. Because of the inherent anonymity of the internet, people often lose social inhibitions and act in ways they would never act in person. In the name of promoting an agenda, we inadvertently create divisiveness and provoke resentment. We are fueling a culture of attacking and slamming.

Although there are extreme instances of racism from truly bigoted people, the bar for what has been considered racist has dropped so low that it seems we are confusing microaggressions for outright racism. In my view, microaggressions are common remarks or perceived human mistakes that should not be interpreted as hostile or incendiary. For example, if someone told me I speak great English, that could be perceived as a microaggression. Personally, I'd view that as a compliment, but many others would be offended and call that person a bigot for saying such a thing. Really? All it takes is one wrong word or mistake to become a racist? If that's the case, then most of us would be racists!

What is so concerning about this situation is that there seems to be no consequence for calling someone a racist or a bigot, so long as it is done in the name of stopping insensitivity. Ironically, many of the people who brand others as racists are being hypocritically insensitive by making false accusations without thought of consequence or consideration for the other side.

We can't have a tipped scale while asserting and pushing for a diverse society. Allegorically, we seem to have recreated a modern-day Salem witch trial wrapped around racial insensitivity. In truth, we have no way of knowing what's going on inside another person's head, let alone our own.

Trust and Distrust

One of the greatest human desires is to be trusted. When it comes to furthering equality and justice, we are fighting two polarizing mindsets: trust and distrust. To put it frankly, we are living with an underlying supposition that people cannot be trusted to act fairly toward minorities without enforcement measures. There is the belief that if we do not enforce racial quotas or uphold political correctness, diversity may be in danger of sliding backward. Minorities do not trust that the majority will treat them fairly if these measures are to be removed, while the majority feels handcuffed and resentful for not being trusted and therefore equally distrustful. Both sides are building a great amount of distrust while more and more resentment spreads underneath.

In a *Harvard Business Review* article, "Why Diversity Programs Fail," Frank Dobbin, sociology professor at Harvard, and Alexandra Kalev, associate professor of sociology at Tel Aviv University, explain why traditional diversity efforts have not worked. In the past thirty years (1985–2014), among all American companies with one hundred or more employees, the proportion of black men working in management roles increased only from 3 percent to 3.3 percent. The proportion of white women in management roles saw bigger gains from 1985 to 2000 (22 percent to 29 percent) but that group has not increased significantly since then.[2]

According to the article, intervention tools to reduce bias on the job include mandatory diversity training, hiring tests, performance ratings, and grievance systems. "Despite a few new bells and whistles . . . companies are doubling down on the same approaches they've used since the 1960s. . . . [Diversity] tools are designed to pre-empt lawsuits by policing managers' thoughts and actions. Yet laboratory studies show that this kind of force-feeding can activate bias rather than stamp it out. . . . [You] won't get managers on board by blaming and shaming them with rules and re-education."

I am not surprised by the results and conclusions of the article. Through my years of living and working in the United States, I have experienced from friends, colleagues, and acquaintances of all races widespread cynicism and antipathy toward diversity mandates that do not take into account human feelings and reactions toward controls and distrust. I witnessed some people take advantage of the system, many others react with resentment and frustration, and still others go through the motions to avoid legal implications.

As a culture, our collective mindsets and attitudes shift over time. Living in a climate of distrust can move us forward only so far. Imagine raising a child without any sense of trust, only with strict rules, negative reinforcement, and repression of thoughts and emotions. You may get short-term results, but sooner or later that child will rebel with built-up anger and resentment, just like we saw in the 2016 presidential election. Many people who voted for Trump disliked Trump, but voted for him as a backlash against our politically correct culture and racial distrust. A vote for Trump was a symbolic rebellion against the straitjacket many people felt they were trapped inside.

Is forced diversity real diversity? It would be advantageous to pause and question whether we are really embracing true diversity or if we are just following rules and political correctness. The reality is that the line between the racial majority and racial minority will eventually disappear, as America is becoming more diverse every day. America has moved from a dominantly homogenous society to that of a multiracial and multicultural melting pot. Based on the National Center for Biotechnology Information (NCBI) data, in 1960, all minorities consisted of approximately 11 percent of the total US population.[3] In 2020, the minority population is projected to account for 39.9 percent, and by 2042, 50.1 percent, according to the US Census Bureau.[4] We will come to a point at which we will ask ourselves what a minority is in 21st-century

America. This is not a matter of politics; it's a matter of science.

Fairness Trade-Offs

As our current diversity practice and mindset continues, we should ask controversial and difficult questions: "Is our diversity framework as relevant today as it was thirty years ago?" "Does our diversity practice beget fairness in today's world or are we tipping the scale?" "Is it possible that our diversity framework may lead to furthering attitudes of discrimination or entitlement?" "Does anyone feel safe or comfortable raising these questions openly in today's politically correct climate?"

We live in an ever-increasing multiracial and multicultural milieu with shifting values and perspectives. As the composition of the US population changes, our mindsets shift as well, especially among the young. I see a clear evolution of progressive changes in mindsets and social behaviors in our younger generations. The environment that young adults and teenagers are brought up in is very conducive to diversity in thought, new perspectives, and open-mindedness.

In today's internet era, younger generations are more exposed to and connected with different ideas, thoughts, cultures, and approaches to life than previous generations. On the flip side, the internet can also fuel hate, narrow-mindedness, and instill righteousness; it just depends on how one uses the internet—to expand one's perspective or to reinforce what you already believe. In this mixed environment, young generations are constantly being asked to label and define themselves in academic and work settings, just like older generations. By defining themselves by race and labels, younger generations are brought up under the narrowly defined diversity framework. Skin color, race, and ethnicity, rather than inclusion, are constantly being reinforced.

In 1961, affirmative action was absolutely necessary in a world full of blatant and widespread discrimination against blacks and other minority groups. But 2020 is a far cry from where we were in 1961. Are we perfect today? Absolutely not. But should we still enforce affirmative action as though we are still living in 1960s America? Our country has made tremendous strides to provide opportunities and social mobility to those who are marginalized. However, as we move into changing demographics, shifting values and attitudes, and heightened racial dividedness, adhering to preferential treatments for minority groups may no longer be as relevant or effective. Race, ethnicity, and gender are now out-valuing achievement, merit, and talent.

We often hear that someone was accepted into an Ivy League university or was promoted only because he or she is a minority. We should not think this way. It's a major problem when a minority individual who is truly accomplished has to wonder: was it me or was it the system? This takes away from one's hard work, confidence, and dignity. On the flip side, those who are not labeled as a minority but who worked very hard and received rejection may become resentful and wonder if their failure was due to the system and not their effort. Instead of nurturing trust in the system, our system breeds resentment, distrust, and an unfair emphasis on race. Are we really rewarding those who work hard regardless of race, gender, or ethnicity?

The purpose of affirmative action was to encourage racial and gender diversity, not to entitle it. When race, ethnicity, and gender become qualifications and out-value achievement, merit, and talent, we do not advance fairness and equality; we build anger and divides. Additionally, many young-adult minorities come from well-to-do families from high socioeconomic brackets. Are we really being fair to those who are truly in financial need regardless of their race?

True diversity is not about separating people through racial labeling, political correctness, or forcing behaviors and outcomes. Diversity is about bringing a multitude of people with vastly different histories, backgrounds, mindsets, attitudes, and cultures under one umbrella. We all want to belong, whether that is in a family, a community, a workplace, or a nation. Diversity issues are complex and multifaceted, and there are no simple solutions. We may not be able to entirely rid the world of racial divisions and tensions, but we can strive for a better world.

We have reached a critical point at which we must seek alternative methods to reduce racial division and augment comfortable integration. We must have both: changes in the system and changes in people. We need bold changes in the current systems and social climate that can encourage broader perspectives and behavioral shifts. At the same time, we ought to also acknowledge the reality that laws or rules may drive certain behaviors, but they will not alter human nature or individual mindsets.

Shifting mindsets is the ultimate producer of lasting change. True change happens in the mind, and if we change the way we look at one another, we can change the way we look at diversity. If we want genuine diversity, we must strike a balance between enforcement and voluntary embracement that comes without even thinking about it.

Essential Takeaways

- If humans constantly evolve and mindsets and attitudes shift with time, then our diversity perspectives and policies should evolve as well. In the face of mounting challenges, our system remains static, and focuses on racial statistical metrics and enforcements.
- Individual perspectives and feelings drive inclusiveness far more than systems or compliance measures. If we can accept this human reality, we can start to evaluate and develop diversity programs from a different angle. We can begin to infuse a human element: increase those that connect, and decrease those that divide.
- One of the greatest human needs is to be heard. Diversity strategies that implement people's feelings, attitudes, needs, and voices foster an atmosphere in which every individual is made to feel that they belong. In workplaces, this approach will bolster dialogues, collaboration, fulfillment, and business results, and reduce politically correct guardedness, silent resentments, fears, and resistance.

9

PERVASIVE DIVERSITY

Changing Diversity Culture

We accept the fact that every human being possesses a unique set of fingerprints, yet we still struggle to accept differences in race, color, and culture. Why do we choose to treat one another differently because of physical attributes when we already know that we are all uniquely different? Despite our physical differences, we are remarkably similar. While no two humans are identical, we share universal human psychology and 99.5 percent of the same DNA. There is nothing that should keep us separate, and yet many still feel the need to discriminate.

Today, the racial tension that we experience, in addition to political correctness and labeling, leads us to become more color conscious, not color neutral. If one can become color neutral, race and skin pigment become irrelevant, and all that matters is the person standing before you. It may sound contradictory to say that I simultaneously see and do not see skin color, ethnicity, or external differences when meeting new people. It's not that I don't see physical differences; it's just that I don't find these differences relevant in my interactions with people.

When the word *diversity* evokes feelings of connection and embracement, not obligation and tension, that is the sign of true pervasive diversity—a physical and mental space where idealism and reality intersect. In this space, our perception of similarities outweighs our perception of differences. Through the lens of pervasive diversity, we can start to see people beyond labels, categorizations, and stereotypes. We will start to share our viewpoints and perspectives without fear of being demonized, which makes political correctness irrelevant. We will start to collaborate rather than divide, and find a middle ground instead of constantly swinging to the extreme left or the extreme right. In this space, trust prevails over distrust, common human essences eclipse differences, and every race matters equally. While this may sound like an unrealistic and unreachable ideal, what other alternatives do we have?

The Race Box

Where do we begin our journey toward pervasive diversity? As the Chinese philosopher Lao Tzu said, "A journey of a thousand miles begins with a single step." There are many contributors that have led to our highly agitated social climate that we must examine.

If I had to pick the most pivotal place to begin, it would be a reduction of racial labeling. It wouldn't be an overstatement to say that the race box—the US Census Bureau's adherence to race and ethnicity classification found in almost every application—has been the most widespread and intrusive medium that has prolonged racial labeling. I am sure you are familiar with the race box because it has been used in academia, testing, jobs, mortgage applications, opinion polls, and much more.

Although my proposal may seem outlandish, imagine if we never had to check this box. This is not to say that there isn't an importance with statistical racial data, but there are unintended consequences that manifest when people start to identify themselves within a small box. Every time a person is asked to check their race, that person is being asked to self-identify and define who they are through a narrow dimension: race and ethnicity. The more people see themselves inside a box, the less they can think outside of it. We are so much bigger than a box and to reduce one's identity to a single characteristic is limiting to who we are.

This is not to say we should get rid of the race box entirely. The importance of US census data can't be overestimated. The first recorded use of the "race box" was in 1790 for the first-ever US census. At the time, there were only five boxes to pick from: Free White males of sixteen years of age, Free White males under sixteen years of age, Free White females, All other free persons, and Slave.[1] Census data is used by various agencies to monitor and enforce civil rights laws. The data allow us to obtain critical information on our nation, our people, and our economy. Census data provide us with demographic information, determine the allocation of the US House of Representatives seats, and help decide how to distribute federal funds to local, state, and tribal governments each year.

Despite the many practical applications that result from race box statistics, the race box puts people into a physical and mental box that labels individuals, accentuates differences, and builds separateness. Over time the race box has been a powerful subliminal catalyst that reinforces America's way of thinking, seeing, and describing people primarily based on race and skin color. Each time I had to check the race box through my years in the United States, I felt resentment at being reduced into a single category. I know that I am not the only one who feels this way.

The more we check these boxes, the more the boxes become part of us. Compounding the emotional issues with the box is that many people are skeptical and suspicious of it. They wonder: How is this data being used? Why does it matter? Will it help me or hurt me? Some people manipulate and change their answers, as we see in job and college applications, to use their racial background as a leg up against the competition. For example, a B+ student who is majority Asian and partially Native American may have an easier time gaining acceptance into college by applying as a full Native American.

Imagine weaning off the widespread practice of the race box. At first, it may create considerable havoc and doubt. People may feel the opposite of my intention—feeling as though their race is being ignored or that we may undo years of progress. They may argue that we are becoming insensitive toward racial differences and do not care. On the other hand, decreasing the use of the race box may be seen as a powerful metaphor: the removal of our rigid attachment to race and preferential racial treatment. It may be liberating. Before we can take a stance on one side or the other, we must consider what we are facing today.

We are seeing majority/minority population shifts, a less-than-desirable diversity enforcement track record, and frighteningly high racial divides. By reducing the use of the race box, over time, we may be able to decrease racial stereotyping and promote a fair playing field not based on race but rather on financial need. Why should a less qualified wealthy minority student get preferential treatment over a more qualified poor majority student? Gradually, we will bring a positive shift in the way we think and look at race, and how we think about diversity.

Living beyond labels doesn't mean getting rid of labeling or the race box entirely, which wouldn't be constructive. Rather, the question would be: where do we do less and where do we continue? Any change from the status quo that we have been accustomed to for years is a difficult task. Instituting the necessary measures to move closer to pervasive diversity will entail changes in diversity systems, more courageous leadership, and behavior shifts.

No Box to Find a Home

Contrary to the belief, the race box can actually deny opportunities and hold us back. This could have been the case for a Brazilian friend of mine, Isabella. In 1974, when Isabella was only six years old, her mother left her at the local Catholic church. Isabella's single mother couldn't afford to raise her daughter and decided to give her up for adoption. Because Brazil didn't have a welfare system for children, the church sent Isabella to The New York Foundling, one of New York City's oldest and largest nonprofit organizations, whose mission was to be a home for abandoned children.

Isabella is a mixed child, with a white Italian mother and a black Brazilian father. Needless to say, Isabella was heartbroken by her mother's decision to leave her. Nonetheless, her strong young heart had great hope that The Foundling would be able to find her a new home. When Isabella arrived, the first thing she had to do was fill out paperwork and check the race box. As a half-Italian, half-black Brazilian girl, there was no box for a mixed child such as Isabella. Customarily, The Foundling presented infants and young children to prospective parents who requested their preferences according to the list of the specific race boxes. By not being able to fill out the racial category, Isabella was not shown to prospective American families for adoption, even if there were parents who would have wanted a mixed child.

Knowing Isabella, who is gorgeous inside and out, I can only imagine what a beautiful and lovely little girl she must have been. Not knowing what to do about Isabella, The Foundling placed her with the disabled children. For one year, Isabella sat by the doors, praying that a good family would soon want her. One day, her dream came true. A British couple who worked in Princeton, New Jersey, was looking to adopt a child before returning to London. They wanted to visit the disabled children and when they entered, they spotted Isabella. They fell in love with Isabella and adopted her on the spot. She grew up in London with her new loving family, eventually attended college in Cambridge, England, and landed a successful career in dance and entertainment.

Early Conditioning

To this day, my daughter, Sophia, still remembers her first encounter with the race box. As a second-grader in the mid-1990s, Sophia was asked to check the box on her Educational Record Bureau admission test. She didn't see a box that described her, being half-white and half-Asian. She was confused and frustrated that she didn't fit into any category. She started to wonder, "What am I? Where do I fit in?" She thought, "Maybe I should check both white and Asian boxes," but didn't know if that was allowed. She then thought about checking the white box, but realized, "I am more than just white . . . I'm German and Welsh."

The race box instills the awareness of racial identity early on in children's minds. They are being conditioned to label and identify themselves, as well as others, by race. Without being conscious of it, children begin the process of separation, not connection. In my daughter's case, she began to feel marginalized for not being able to find a box that matched her, besides the box labeled "Other."

According to the US Census Bureau, the mixed-race population (two or more races), including children such as Isabella and Sophia, is projected to be the fastest-growing demographic group in the US.[2] This trend supports the increasing multiracial milieu we live in and as a result there will be more interracial marriages. It also illustrates how our current practice of drawing race distinctions does not align with the future direction of our nation.

In the 2010 US census, the "Some Other Race" category was the third-largest at 6.2 percent of the population.[3] To reduce "Other" and improve the accuracy of its race and ethnicity data, the Census Bureau is in the process of finding alternative ways of identifying those with mixed backgrounds.[4] Could this also mean that there will be an increased number of boxes to accommodate changing demographics? The US Census Bureau conducts its survey every ten years; its low frequency lags behind our quickly evolving world. However, if we were to adopt their revised race boxes in the future, we will only be dissecting races into an increased number of labels and separations. What would be the impact of using the race box that will be even more divided in our daily lives if we hope to mitigate the downsides of labeling and advance pervasive diversity?

Personal Agendas: Closed Eyes and Closed Ears

When one is consumed by forwarding personal gains and motives, it's nearly impossible to keep clarity of thought. In the process, alternate possibilities that may be more conducive to advancing progress may be overlooked. We see this in partisan politics: one side not willing to give an inch, which results in a lose-lose situation. We see this form of human righteousness and emotional rigidity everywhere, from our biased news media, riots, mob mentality, social justice warriors, the alt-right, the radical-left, and in everyday conversations that can lead to blowups and damaged relationships. A parallel that powerfully portrays this sentiment can be found in the

1952 French novel *The Bridge over the River Kwai,* which was famously adapted in the 1957 Academy Award Best Picture winner.

The Bridge over the River Kwai is a timeless classic about a British colonel who is taken as prisoner of war during World War II. He is forced to oversee the construction of a railway bridge to aid in the war efforts of his Japanese captors. The colonel, lost in his love for building a beautifully designed and engineered bridge, obstructed the Allies' efforts to destroy it. Blinded by his own agenda, he couldn't see the consequences of his actions, losing grasp of the bigger picture of winning the war. *The Bridge over the River Kwai* speaks as powerfully today as it did in 1952 about blinding personal agendas.

We have become a culture in which people's perspectives are so polarized that it has become extremely difficult to share opposing thoughts or values in a productive dialogue. The matter is most fraught when we talk about race. It's one thing to bring awareness to social and diversity issues and promote messages that have the power to shift mindsets and make differences; it's another to attack, alienate, condemn, or shame those who do not share the same agenda. With this stance, there is no room for dialogue or to be open to differences, alternatives, or consensus. Righteousness is not progressive. When we exhibit extreme divisiveness and hostility to uphold our own personal agendas, we are indirectly endorsing and spreading an unhealthy social climate and cultural norm. In this atmosphere, how could we as a nation possibly pursue pervasive diversity that nurtures connection and unity?

A Future Without Blame or Guilt

In Chapter 2, I told the story of Hiya, the maid who served my family from the age of twelve, with whom I built a lifelong sisterhood bond. Hiya was the victim of unfortunate circumstances beyond her control. In my early years, I didn't have the resources to articulate my feelings about my relationship with Hiya.

In reflection, I carried a convoluted mixture of guilt, arrogance, prejudice, love, and a sense of equality. I felt guilty about my privilege; however, I also detected her underlying resentment and anger toward me. The more resentment I perceived from her, the more I did to try to compensate for her lack of fortune. In secrecy, I gave her some of my clothes, extra money, and material help whenever I could. I felt this gesture would help heal her pain and free me from my guilt. Little did I know, I was actually putting her down by making her feel even worse about her circumstances.

Although my initial intention was to empower her, I learned that I was doing the exact opposite. Hiya told me that what made a real difference in her life was not the material goods I gave her; it was the way I treated her—as being my equal with love and respect. What she wanted more than anything was equality and the opportunity for a better life. I learned that no amount of material items could compensate for her loss of hope and dignity.

Hiya taught me that genuine love and equality must transcend the act of giving based on guilt or a sense of arrogance. I felt good about helping Hiya, but I was boosting my ego by "doing the right thing" and therefore believing I was a good person. I learned that giving is not necessarily sharing. We like to pat ourselves on the back for helping the less fortunate, but if all we are doing is boosting our own ego, then what we are giving ends up being superficial, and those who receive will feel it. I learned that if I truly felt that Hiya was my equal, I could not possibly possess any hint of superiority or guilt. When we respect and embrace others without any distinction from ourselves, that is when we truly connect and can make a real difference in someone else's life.

I think about my conversation with Jodie about reparations, and I realize there is circumstantial resemblance between Hiya's situation and those of oppressed black slaves. I ask: Did I cause harm to Hiya? Should I be punished for thinking our young maids and Hiya were lucky and I was superior to them? Should I be punished for my older family members utilizing young labor more than sixty years ago in a different time and place? I am not the same person today as I was growing up. If I were to still punish myself, what means would be appropriate? Should I feel guilty forever or for a set period of time? How long exactly? Who would gain from this? What could be lost? Instead, wouldn't it be better if Hiya and I (if she were alive) moved forward, striving together toward a better place with expanded empathy and making changes that will affect the future?

Hiya helped me understand firsthand, albeit on a minute scale, the downward cycle of an entangled knot of guilt and anger. I see this complex and difficult human dynamic of guilt and anger in the larger racial and political divide in America today. I don't believe we can move our society toward one that is interlaced with the essence of pervasive diversity by dwelling in the past with guilt and anger. We must honor and embrace our ever-changing present to shape our shared future. We cannot change the past; we can only change the future. Guilt doesn't move us forward; instead, it prolongs a culture of victimization that does not produce empowerment, openness, or optimism, but rather resentment and pessimism. When blame and anger hurt everyone, no one benefits.

Empathy

If we hope to achieve pervasive diversity, empathy is a key element to foster. While it's easy to say we must be more empathic to one another, it's difficult to relate to things that we haven't experienced—be it culture, socio-economics, education, upbringing, or beliefs. While it's important to have empathy for those who have dealt with unfortunate circumstances such as starvation or extreme prejudice, it's impossible to know how that person feels without being that person.

You may ask: Is it even possible to acquire empathy without sharing the same experience? Of course it is. Empathy isn't about sharing a mutual experience; it's about possessing kindness, openness, and the willingness to listen to and learn about others. The connecting force of empathy is the opposite of the disconnecting force of judging oneself or others.

To deepen our capacity for empathy, we have to be willing to step into another person's shoes without judging. No two people share the same life, yet our physical sensations and emotions are universal: hunger, pain, relief, love, despair, anger, shame, jealously, happiness, regret, and fear. No matter how much I wanted to feel for Hiya, I never could have entirely understood the excruciating hunger pangs or despair she experienced. While it's impossible to fully relate to another person, it's very possible to expand our awareness and develop empathy.

For example, we have all experienced hunger. Sometimes we miss lunch due to a busy schedule or have to fast for a medical procedure. Imagine living with that hunger for days without any hope. Although we may never have experienced true starvation, by using our imagination, we can expand our empathy to those who have had to live with perpetual hunger. By stretching our imagination, we can take a glimpse into the state of mind of those less fortunate. If you've ever been brought to tears while watching a movie, then you've already done this. We may be sitting in the comfort of our own homes, watching an interpretation of an event portrayed by actors on a set, but we still find ourselves moved. What happens in a movie never actually happened, but we feel like it did. The great film critic Roger Ebert once said: "The movies are like a machine that generates empathy. It lets you understand a little bit more about different hopes, aspirations, dreams, and fears. It helps us to identify with people who are sharing this journey with us."

By enlarging our imagination, we can enter a new world and connect through the power of empathy. Empathy is not about feeling guilt or pity. We often see empathy being used as a political tactic to sway and alter one's position. While we can listen, understand, and empathize with others, we can still hold true to our own beliefs.

Self-Righteousness

Four of the worst words we can say to ourselves are "I already know that." When we say this self-righteous phrase, we close ourselves off from new opportunities. A quality that prevents pervasive diversity, righteousness lies on the opposite end of the spectrum from empathy. Righteousness leads to defensiveness and blaming; neither attitude will result in one's growth or connection, and both stop dialogues from progressing.

As equally harmful and self-righteous as saying "I already know that" is "No, you're wrong." This saying is the ultimate relational corruptor; it will repel others from any desire to connect. Self-righteous people do not hear others, and they blame others since they cannot be wrong. We see the damaging effects of righteousness in all arenas of life, from politics to business, from the progressive left to the conservative right. There is a difference between being passionate about what we believe in and disregarding others' views. Rumi, a 13th-century Islamic poet, wrote the following:

> Out beyond ideas of wrongdoing and rightdoing,
> there is a field. I'll meet you there.

This beautiful phrase perfectly illustrates where our perspective needs to be to broaden, grow, and connect: beyond right and wrong. If we hope to achieve pervasive diversity, we must be open to examining our mindsets and attitudes toward differences. Pervasive diversity requires our willingness to look past our own realities and consider others' realities. We must remember that there are many worlds that exist out there beyond our own. Developing the flexibility to overcome the urge to be right frees us from a narrowly confined world with limited possibilities.

The Wisdom of Children: Innate Pervasive Diversity

Children naturally operate in pervasive diversity. They don't focus on differences as adults do. They welcome and connect from their hearts. They don't label or judge based on race or skin color, unless they are taught otherwise. And certainly they do not think about political correctness. There is so much we can learn from children: the way they think, act, and love the world around them. We were all once little children; so what happened to us?

One summer in the late 1990s, my husband and I took both our children, Sophia and Michael (ten and eight years old, respectively), to visit South Korea. I always found it interesting that in Asia, people see our children more as Westerners, while in America, people see them more as Asians. In the 1990s, anything from American culture was idolized in many Asian cultures.

My children couldn't believe how much American influence had been injected into South Korean society. My kids' favorite TV shows were all on Korean TV (*The Simpsons*, *WWF Wrestling*, Disney movies); fast-food chains such as KFC, Dunkin' Donuts, and McDonald's were commonplace; and many signs and posters around Seoul were written in English, which made getting around town easy.

One day during our visit, we took our children to a farming area far from Seoul. As we were walking through a park, a mob of Korean schoolchildren on a field trip saw our children and flocked over instantly. They surrounded Sophia and Michael in fascination, taking pictures and asking for their autographs! The schoolchildren were extremely excited to encounter kids of their age who, in their eyes, were Westerners.

Surrounded by dozens of Korean children, my children felt awkward about the celebrity-like attention they received. Despite their differences, our children and the Koreans immediately shared a youthful delight over this encounter and embraced one another. They couldn't communicate through language, as our children spoke only English. Nonetheless, it was touching to witness this joyful interaction between two different worlds connected by open hearts. Visible differences in others are always far more noticeable than what's not shown. Yet children have an uncanny instinct to transcend external differences and connect. If we could preserve this wisdom throughout life, we would all be living in a much more unified world.

There is a funny expression that states, "You will never know more than you do at eighteen." I believe you will never know more than when you are eight! While we may not have accumulated knowledge or life experience at eight years old, our young hearts are innately wiser and unjaded compared to how they will be in our adult years. No one is born a bully, and yet we still witness young children who become bullies due to their inherited imprints. For the most part, you don't often see children on the playground having a hard time making friends or reaching out to others. They don't judge each other the way adults do. They don't have built-up concepts of biases or prejudice until later in life. Embracing pervasive diversity is innate in all of us. Can we work on bringing back our heart of openness and acceptance of others as we once had?

A Road Not Forced

There are two kinds of people: bamboos and willow trees. Bamboos are strong and stable but snap easily due to their rigidity. Willow trees are soft and flexible but sway uncontrollably because they have no backbone. One's strength is the other's weakness.

I grew up hearing this helpful adage from my parents and I still see this sentiment as a useful metaphor for temperament and balance in all people. It teaches us that our mindsets should be somewhere in the middle, between rigidity and flexibility, so that we can live in balance, with reduced pressures and tensions. When we are dealing with diversity and promoting change, it is inevitable that we can be overwhelmed by a wide range of emotions. Making progress is not about swinging the pendulum from one side to the other, nor is it about imposing one's values righteously.

Throughout history, humans have had a difficult time finding balance, individually and collectively. I grew up with the fundamental principle of yin and yang, the Chinese philosophy and culture that all things exist in intrinsic dualities (moon and sun, passive and aggressive, feminine and masculine, and so on). Opposite forces are contradictory yet inseparable, such as how lightness exists in the dark, and darkness exists in light. It says that to achieve harmony, we must strive for the correct balance between two opposites. As a society, we will never be able to cooperate without balancing the forces of opposing sides. We cannot bend too far, and yet we cannot snap through our rigidity. To attain pervasive diversity and social harmony, we need to embrace the reality that we have to work with each other.

We all have constructed our own inner borders through our vastly different scripts, upbringings, and experiences. Some of our internal borders are solid and unyielding as steel. For others, they are more permeable. Not everyone will choose to go along with changes or accept others who are different. Accepting others doesn't mean becoming like them or being their friends. It's not about going outside of our comfort zone or condoning actions that do not align with our values. Rather, it's about embracing our humanity, broadening our horizons, and having nonjudgmental flexibility. And for some, acceptance might mean raising the threshold for their tolerance.

Regardless of the varying degrees of our inner worlds, the more of us that take steps toward accepting differences, the sooner we will ride the tide of change. We will gradually propagate new societal norms. We will in time move past what limits us, to living in harmony and in pervasive diversity. Our accepting mindsets and attitudes will become second nature, in the same way most of us say "please" and "thank you" automatically.

Essential Takeaways

- If we aspire for a more authentic and healthier diversity climate for us and for our children, then our focus shouldn't be about creating more mandates, statistics, or old paradigms that we know don't serve us. What we need are more neutral lenses and the resolve to regard others as equals beyond external characteristics.

- In pervasive diversity, everyone matters equally. Americans have been indoctrinated to view diversity as a way to group people based on race. Any measures and behaviors that exclude, divide, or alienate, such as race boxes, racial labeling, and preferential treatments evoke anger and ruptures, dampening good will and advancements.
- A diversity culture is an amalgamation and manifestation of how we all collectively feel inside. Sustainable changes must come from a voluntary embracement of humanity that arises out of one's heart. When we act from our heart, it becomes part of our fabric and we can start doing it without thinking.

10

UNIFYING LEADERSHIP

How Our Leaders Can Help

In a world where we are challenged by racial tensions, polarizing politics, and multiculturalism, we are hungry for great leaders. According to a Gallup poll conducted in July 2020, 77 percent of Americans disapproved of the US Congress. In the past ten years (July 2010–July 2020), Congress's job disapproval rate ranged between 65 percent and 86 percent.[1] When leaders do not garner respect, they do not inspire. When leaders do not inspire, we all suffer.

In our time of sharply heightened public concern over race relations, it is crucial to have leadership that can help cultivate an authentic path to diversity. Our lives are to a great extent affected by how our leaders think and what they do. A country's unity or divide rides on the mindsets and actions of its leaders, whether they be in government, business, or academics. They exert a pivotal role in our diversity journey toward healing and harmony as they set policies and directions that touch our daily lives.

They shape the tone for their country and organizations and influence the climate of the community they lead through their intrinsic energy and presence.

It wouldn't be possible to advance pervasive diversity without leaders who are committed toward making bold (not necessarily popular) changes. Leaders have the ability to unify and advance the health of society or workplace as well as the power to corrode the culture and people within it. Sadly, we too often see leaders who are more concerned with winning or being re-elected that they'll trade "doing the right thing" for "winning at all costs." We see this not only in politics, but in all fields. Most people will do anything to keep their jobs, no matter the cost.

Leaders are bestowed with the privilege to inspire others and implement reforms that ultimately make real changes in people's lives. Great leaders bring out their true selves through their actions and behaviors that touch and move people. While a leader is only one person in an ocean of individuals, for better or worse, leaders have the power to influence mindsets to a greater degree than any other force. No one can change our mind other than ourselves, but that's not to say we cannot be influenced.

The influencing effect leaders have on individuals can foster a multiplying effect that spreads to that person's loved ones, family, friends, and society. With such solemn privilege and responsibility given to them, leaders are accountable to examine the basis of their motivations and agendas and to reflect on the potential outcomes they may strive toward. Their ambitions and efforts can lead society toward two divergent paths: pushing for divides and anger, or promoting healing and unity.

Leadership is given; great leadership must be earned. Sadly, many leaders throughout history have abused their privilege, usurped by the greed of power. Unfortunately, greed and power are enduring human vices that will never go away. Trying to remove the world of greed would be as difficult as removing the world of happiness. Nonetheless, integrity and altruism are also inherent human characteristics. We see both sides with leaders, sometimes both within the same person. Could there be a leader who can completely transcend the negative side of being human? That's doubtful. To me, it's not all or none, it's about what degree, to what cost, and to what benefit.

The Demise of a Patriot

Power corrupts. The greater power one yields, the greater destruction one can leave behind. On April 19, 1960, nearly 200 students were killed and thousands were injured during a massive political protest against South Korea's first president, Syngman Rhee. Agitated by the rigged presidential election the month before, Koreans were fed up with the corrupt regime. The massive riot, culminating with a demonstration of more than 100,000 students and protesters, successfully brought an end to Rhee's leadership.

Originally loved and respected by the people, Rhee had led the country from 1945 until his fall on April 26, 1960. He was a conservative patriot, a staunch anti-communist, and an esteemed authoritarian who fervently fought for independence from Japan's colonization of Korea (1910–1945). Backed by the United States, President Rhee had begun a promising new era for South Korea. Sadly, his regime took a turn for the worse as he became increasingly dictatorial and corrupt. After serving three terms, Rhee blatantly rigged the vote and stole his fourth election, infuriating the Korean public.

During the infamous bloody demonstration known as the April Revolution, Rhee imposed a state of martial law and ordered his police force and army to contain the demonstrators by any means necessary, including firing at the unarmed protesters. My father, a military general at the time, was never put into a position like the one he found himself in: torn between the orders of his superiors and doing what he knew in his heart was right. He always believed in putting his country first, and in this case, that meant disobeying his leaders. Rather than obeying Rhee's orders, my father refused to open fire on the demonstrating students. Instead, he enforced a cease-fire and protected the students.

The next day, my father was summoned by President Rhee. He knew disobeying the president's orders could lead to a severe punishment, and he expected to be stripped of his military rank by a court-martial. When my father walked in, Rhee looked my father in the eye and said, "I wanted to meet the young general who had the stomach to disobey me." Rather than destroying my father's military career, Rhee was impressed by my father's courage in taking a stand for justice. I can't help but feel that Rhee saw himself in this young general, the courage to do the right thing even in the face of death, even if that part of Rhee was long gone.

Although my father felt a sense of anguish and betrayal over Rhee's fall into corruption, he was still moved by this encounter. After Rhee fell from power, he was ultimately exiled to Hawaii, where he lived the rest of his life in isolation and disgrace. In stark contrast to his reign, during which people literally kissed his feet, no one visited the former president in Hawaii; there would be no political gain in doing so. It was a tragic end for a leader who once did so much good for his country but who lost his way through corruption and power. My father, out of his loyalty to the human being Rhee once embodied, was the only high-ranking political figure who went to pay his respects to Rhee before he died in 1965.

Leadership requires the courage and integrity to take a stand for what truly matters and the discipline to transcend the temptations of greed for power. One moment, Rhee was the most powerful man in South Korea, with legions of followers and kowtowing subordinates. The next, he was a pariah, abandoned by his supporters once he was no longer useful to them. President Rhee took his people and the country down with him. As he succumbed to corruption and power, Rhee forgot who he was serving and the people who had faith in him. Sadly, we still see examples of leaders abusing their power and falling victim to their own corruption.

Power: An Intoxicating Destroyer

Any man can withstand adversity; if you want to test his character, give him power.

—Abraham Lincoln

Power is intoxicating; no one is above it. Power can be put to good use, but I have also seen the destructive nature of power at every level of organizations, societies, and cultures. From the highest level of government to mom-and-pop businesses, from churches to not-for-profit entities, the more authority and power one possesses, the more abuse one may inflict; it's in our nature. For leaders, abuse of power is the fastest and surest way to lose connection with themselves, and therefore, with those who they lead.

The Stanford Prison Experiment in 1971, theorized and led by Dr. Philip Zimbardo, was one of the most groundbreaking and disturbing psychological studies on human behavior ever conducted.[2] Zimbardo wanted to study the psychological effects of a prison environment. Out of seventy-five undergraduate candidates at Stanford University, Dr. Zimbardo selected twenty-four students who were considered the most psychologically stable and healthy to participate in his experiment. For the study, Zimbardo created a mock prison beneath the university. By flipping a coin, half of the students were assigned to play guards, the other half prisoners.

Originally, the study was designed to last two weeks, but it was stopped after only six days due to the severe emotional and physical distress inflicted onto the prisoners by the guards. In that short amount of time, the college students' perspectives quickly became distorted. Video surveillance footage documented the entire study and the shocking results were all captured on tape. The guards started to abuse their power, use verbal insults, and inflict emotional distress and physical violence. The prisoners attempted to retaliate but quickly became submissive.

The Stanford Prison Experiment demonstrates how good people can do bad things given the right circumstances. The participants all knew this was a simulation with no real-life consequences, yet they were overtaken by the illusion of power and authority. Zimbardo's experiment on the psychology of authority and the abuse of power was a landmark study that changed the perception of human nature.

Absolute power absolutely corrupts. No matter who we are, no matter how good we may be, given enough power, it is easy to lose ourselves and become blind to corruption. As we have seen with President Rhee and the Stanford Prison Experiment, the tendency to do so is pervasive and universal within the human psyche. People often forget that power can be given and usurped, whether large or small, and never lasts forever. When power leads to hubris, it's easy to inflate one's ego with a skewed self-image of oneself and one's surroundings. A leader can become insular and disconnected from reality, and ultimately pay a hefty price for that lack of awareness. Unfortunately, they don't just hurt themselves, they affect many people around them.

Arrogance that stems from a sense of superiority distances people and, worse, creates deep-seated anger and resentment. A leader's responsibility is to be aware of the dark side of human nature and also to realize that the power can be put to good use, rather than abuse. How one exercises and leads with power hinges upon who the leader is as a human being.

A Journey from Ordinary to Extraordinary

Growing up, I was fortunate to be exposed to the government and business leaders with whom my father interacted. The most profound lesson I learned from observing these men and women was that leaders are everyday people, just like you and me, who possess the same human virtues and fallacies we all share. Through deep commitment and hard work, these ordinary people may become extraordinary.

The top priority for any leader is to produce results; regardless of industry or profession, this is the one unifying and nonnegotiable responsibility that all leaders share. When leaders don't generate results, they are unable to gain credibility, respect, or power. Many leaders I experienced, because of time and emotional pressure exerted by their strict mandates, often forewent or ignored the importance of people and humanity. This is an unfortunate oversight that often separates competent and great leaders.

Good leaders produce results. Extraordinary leaders are able to produce results and cultivate human connection that inspires, nourishes, and empowers all those who follow. There is nothing more miserable than following a leader we do not respect or believe in.

Regardless of policy or work ethic, the ability to make genuine connections that touch people is by far the most difficult feat for any leader to accomplish. When leaders connect with genuine hearts, regardless of title, status, or wealth, they create a deep bond and a mutually shared energy that transcends hierarchy and human differences. Great leaders tap into this space and have the power to influence the way others think and feel. When we listen to a leader speak passionately about his or her beliefs, we can feel it in our heart and soul. When someone is manipulative or disingenuous, we can tell the difference.

A leader's ability to connect cannot be manufactured; it must come from within. Through their connecting energy, a force no words can truly describe, great leaders move those who follow and can change the people around them.

From heads of government to CEOs, and from military generals to film directors, having empathy and the ability to connect with others is what truly makes a great leader. Great leaders possess the ability to foster unity and pervasive diversity.

Leaders are not just defined by their popularity or visibility. We cannot forget the countless other great leaders in the world who may not make a Fortune or Forbes list or don't yet have a book written about them. These are the leaders who make a profound impact on individuals' lives every day on a smaller but no less significant scale. They foster human connection and build steps toward pervasive diversity. I am talking about parents, teachers, professors, doctors, nurses, caretakers, therapists, coaches, and everyone in between who makes lasting impacts that change individuals every day.

It is our responsibility to identify and support leaders, whether in the public or private sectors, who we believe will take on the challenges of making bold changes that will put our society on the path toward pervasive diversity and unity. On the surface, many great leaders may not appear to possess all the bells and whistles, yet underneath, they carry the qualities that withstand the temptations of power and greed. They put their people and society before their personal agendas and gains. They inspire us. They help us change and grow. We are eager to find these kinds of leaders. How can we spot them?

What qualities might they bear? I have been fortunate to encounter some of them.

Humility, Confidence, Hierarchy

When I started my business career in the early 1980s, I had an opportunity to meet an incredible American businessman, Tom, who was a corporate officer for a major US multinational corporation. Tom's company had a global presence in more than one hundred countries.

During this era, the pervading sentiment throughout many parts of the world (including South Korea) was that anything from America, even garbage, was golden. United States multinationals yielded great power and influence as well.

That a senior executive would be willing to meet with me—as a beginner entering the business world—felt unreal. For someone as green as I was, meeting with Tom seemed like something out of a dream. Growing up in the extremely hierarchical society of South Korea, I was accustomed to seeing people bow down to my parents in deference. This pervading mentality applied in all aspects of our society—from government and military to school and business.

The possibility didn't even occur to me that Tom, a senior executive, would give me the time of day. Even though I was incredibly nervous about speaking to this man, I was astounded by the way Tom made me feel at ease through his openness and humility. I felt no sense of ego or superiority coming from Tom, just that he respected me as an equal. I immediately felt a genuine connection with him.

Tom shared his philosophy: when we do business abroad, we need to view ourselves as guests in other countries. We have to respect each country's values and cultures. We must try to learn as much as possible and do our best to conduct our affairs in a collaborative manner. We can never act arrogant or assume we know more than they do. Most of all, we must always appreciate the opportunity to be invited to do business in another country.

I've met many leaders who attempt to embody humility and confidence but instead come across as arrogant and contrived. Many inauthentic leaders have to pretend they are humble, while Tom was just effortlessly being who he was. Even in a position of his stature, Tom embodied the perfect blend of authority and humility, a rare quality that is often lost when power gets to people's heads. To find this combination of leadership qualities in one person is rare, but that's exactly what makes a leader great. By balancing power and humility, we can inspire long-lasting impressions and success in any multicultural setting around the world.

As I worked in the US corporate world, I began to absorb the idea that there was a great difference in how hierarchy was viewed and exercised between cultures: a fundamental ethos that separates the East from the West. In many Asian cultures, hierarchy is absolute and governs every domain of life. For example, in South Korea, when a senior member of the family pours a drink, the younger member must hold his or her cup with both hands, turn their body away from the senior member, and drink without making eye contact. This hieratical norm applies everywhere—old and young, teacher and student, parents and children. I doubt many children in America think twice about holding their cups with both hands while their grandparents pour them a drink.

The notion that lower-level employees can interact with the highest level of hierarchy as equals, while still abiding to the corporate ranks, was a foreign idea to me. Looking back at Tom, I still can't believe such a senior-level executive treated me as an equal and gave me the same level of respect as he would to anyone else.

Tom will never know the full extent to which he affected me. In one sitting, he changed my outlook on how I viewed hierarchy, equality, confidence, and arrogance. One of the toughest cultural transitions I had to make was learning to promote myself, particularly in the business environment.

Growing up in South Korea, I was taught to be deferent and humble and to not come across as being too confident, as confidence can be quickly mistaken for arrogance. It didn't take long for me to learn that in the United States, humility can be interpreted as lacking confidence. For example, if you said during an interview in South Korea, "I am great with strategy. I have accomplished many things. I am confident I can do the job better than anyone else," you could be viewed as a buffoon with a big head. In contrast, if you said in an interview in the United States, "I have many areas I'm still improving on. I will try my best to meet your expectations. I will look forward to your guidance and teaching," you could be viewed as weak, lacking assurance and leadership ability.

I was bouncing around between the two polarizing mindsets and behaviors—one that was hammered in by my parents and culture; the other, to act confidently and assertively. As you can imagine, the juggling of these two mindsets led me to overcompensate through unnatural mannerisms and forced actions.

When we come across a new mindset or attitude from what we have been previously accustomed to, we are provided with an opportunity to expand our growth. By connecting beyond the differences in race, culture, and hierarchy, Tom showed me that being humble and confident are not mutually exclusive and that there can be a beautiful harmony when authority, confidence, and humility authentically emanate from within. Without realizing it, Tom helped me broaden my boundaries beyond the beliefs and perspectives I had long held onto. Possessing this powerful capacity to influence and shift others' mindsets is what truly defines a great leader, regardless of one's position in life.

Strength Through Honesty and Vulnerability

In the mid-1990s, I worked under a hard-driving woman who was by far the greatest boss I ever had. A senior corporate officer at a major US corporation, Mary was results-driven, tough, willing to listen, and open to sharing her vulnerabilities. We all loved working for Mary, and each of us would go out of our way to support her, not because we had to, but because of who she was. She inspired us to bring out our best by creating a productive and connected space in which to work.

During that time, Mary told me about a presentation she had made early on in her career. She was meeting with a potential major client. Naturally, she was very nervous and wanted to impress him. This potential client asked what made her believe her proposal was the right one for his company. Rather than overselling in the hope of landing the client, Mary chose to be honest with him, saying she couldn't be completely certain whether her proposal would be the best solution for his company. Nonetheless, she told him what he could always count on was her honesty in answering his questions, no matter what. She promised to do her best to meet his needs by providing the best options her company could devise. Without realizing it, Mary had gained the trust of this potential client, who ended up becoming one of her most loyal customers until he retired twenty-five years later.

There's something I remember one of my business school professors saying many years ago: "Honesty is not the best policy; it's the only policy." It takes a lot of courage to be as honest as Mary was, especially at a junior level, when she was hungry and eager to produce. As a culture, we have become so oversaturated with people trying to sell us that we end up becoming cynical. When people are willing to say anything to make a sale, validity and trust go out the window.

In the heat of the moment, we can often find ourselves acting overly confident to mask our fear. Conventional wisdom equates vulnerability as a weakness, and we resort to lies and false confidence. Many people end up selling smoke and mirrors, instead of actual content. As the sales tactic goes, "Sell the sizzle, not the steak." In reality, showing vulnerability is not a reflection of being emotional or weak; it's about being human. Sometimes the best way to draw people in is not through excessive strength or overt salesmanship. Even if you have to go against what your client may want to hear, being truthful is a powerful connecting force.

As Mary demonstrated, exemplary leaders can be excellent, demanding, and vulnerable all at the same time. The more human we are with one another, the more comfortable we feel. Mary never shied away when she felt vulnerable; instead she openly shared her fears and uncertainties—her true strength. And she never compromised her integrity by letting her vulnerability usurp her honesty. She built relationships founded on trust, loyalty, and collaboration. As a result, Mary ended up being one of the highest-performing executives in the company.

Doing the Work to Change

The ability to face and acknowledge our flaws and weaknesses is one of the most admirable human traits one can possess. Many would rather put up with the consequences of their problem than admit that they have one. Regardless of position or power, it takes an incredible amount of courage and humility to recognize our faults and limitations. It may hurt our egos to admit it, but in the long run, we will ultimately propel our lives to new heights of personal growth.

Terry, a former client of mine, is an exemplary leader who beautifully demonstrates how to overcome the challenge of acknowledging personal flaws and making personal change. Terry had been a senior global executive at one of the top Global 50 corporations for almost thirty years.

I was hired to assess and help expand his leadership growth. To gauge the situation, I conducted feedback interviews with Terry's colleagues, including his manager, his superiors, his peers, and his direct reports. From the responses I received, it was clear Terry had many admirable leadership qualities. People said he had a good heart, was easy to work with, and was open-minded. He was highly regarded, consistently produced excellent results, and was trustworthy. It was a real shock to Terry when he discovered that the number-one area he needed to improve upon was being more respectful of others.

Without being aware of it, Terry's zealousness to produce excellent results came at the cost of his relationships. While Terry was kind and reliable, many felt he micromanaged, didn't listen well, and often came across as disrespectful. Many of Terry's colleagues felt demoralized and disconnected while working with him. Receiving this feedback was painful for Terry to hear, as he believed that being respectful to others was one of the most important human attributes.

Upon hearing my report, he was stunned and felt as though we were talking about a completely different person. Unable to comprehend what I was telling him, he became angry, defensive, and felt undervalued and underappreciated. Terry insisted that I tell him all the names of the people who had provided this feedback, even though he knew that the interview responses were to be kept anonymous.

When he left the office that day, he was fuming in disbelief, but by early the next week, Terry was already making personal changes. It only took one weekend for him to reflect and acknowledge his own part in the problem. One of the first things Terry did upon returning to the office was apologize to his colleagues. He revealed that he was working on his issues and would welcome their continued feedback and support. Before work every morning and before bed every night, Terry reviewed the action plan we devised together and reflected upon his progress.

After six months, I re-interviewed the same people. Across the board, all of Terry's colleagues felt the changes he had made were noticeable and significant. Seeing and experiencing Terry's remarkable change firsthand shifted his colleagues' opinions, and they gained a newfound respect for him. They could feel that his desire to change came from a genuine place. Terry's efforts were not motivated by a should-be leadership development program; they came from deep within his heart.

I have yet to meet a person who does not react defensively upon receiving negative feedback. The pivotal point of moving forward hinges upon how the receiver digests and integrates others' views, especially those opinions that never even crossed one's mind. Not all my clients were as willing to take the necessary steps to make personal change as Terry was. We often heard, "That's not me" or "I never did that" when confronting others with personal assessments.

What made Terry able to move forward was his deep humility in accepting his weaknesses and his strong desire to improve. Like Terry, those who are truly open to others' advice and criticism end up making rewarding shifts in life and at work. Terry inspired others by proving we can change. A leader's willingness to examine and challenge oneself for greater improvement will inspire and motivate others to do the same. As mentioned before, a great leader must lead by example.

What gives great leaders the capacity to deliver, connect, and unify? It is a seemingly simple question that has no simple answer. Great leaders don't force their beliefs on others, but rather embody their intentions and convictions. They manifest their perspectives and humanity in everything they do—making bold changes, influencing mindset, or fostering a unified social climate and culture. Leaders who can connect with others become exemplary for people to want to follow and the integrating force to bring people together.

The title of a leader is not what inspires us, rather it is the person who resides in it. As we look toward our leaders to help bring unity and harmony at large, we cannot forget that as an individual member in our society, we each have the power and responsibility to change and influence a pervasive diversity mindset and culture.

Essential Takeaways

- Leaders must take into their hearts the impact of their mindsets and behaviors, and honor their accountability. Leaders are human, which means that they are fallible. Leadership is about balancing two weights on a scale, taking care of one's self-needs while taking care of others. The needle constantly vacillates. Exemplary leaders are keenly aware of, manage, and grow within this demanding navigation to stay grounded.
- The leadership qualities that connect and bring people together (humility, empathy, open-mindedness,

and courage) can be cultivated in anyone because they are human qualities. Despite the lack of connecting and unifying leaders, we each can be a leader in our lives and workplaces to make a difference.

- Given the opportunity, what one quality would you begin to nurture? How would you go about making that happen?

11

OUR RESPONSIBILITY TO CHANGE

Rewriting Our Scripts

> *A man came upon a construction site where three people were working. He asked the first, "What are you doing?" and the man replied: "I am laying bricks." He asked the second, "What are you doing?" and the man replied: "I am building a wall." As he approached the third, he heard him humming a tune as he worked and asked, "What are you doing?" The man stood, looked up at the sky, and smiled. "I am building a cathedral!"*
>
> —From an 800-year-old parable

I often think back to that moment when I was five years old, staring out through the narrow crack of gate of my home. I find myself wondering how my life would have been different if my father never sprayed me from behind with cold water.

What if instead of jolting me with fear, he opened the doors and let me play outside with the other children? I like to imagine my father smiling, taking hold of my hand, and walking me outside to meet the neighborhood children. I like to imagine saying "hello" to new faces, feeling the rush of excitement from making new friends. I like to imagine my father then inviting my new friends into our house, where they would run around the garden, beaming with joy and laughter. If this actually happened, how would it have changed my life? Would I have grown up with the same feelings of separation, or would I have adopted a new level of openness and empathy?

Pretend for a moment that you can go back in time. What would you do differently? What changes would you wish to make? What would you gain? What changes would be entailed to reshape who you are today? How would you go about it?

A society is made up of individual members. Regardless of who we are, every one of us is a contributor and is accountable for the diversity culture we shape and live in. If we want to shift diversity culture and a sense of racial unity, we have to shift individual mindsets and attitudes toward differences.

Each one of us is the amalgam of all our scripts: old scripts, current scripts, limiting scripts. While we may not be able to time travel, we do have the ability to rewrite scripts and reconstruct who we are at any moment, no matter what age.

Regardless of what change you want to make in your life: self-image, self-empowerment, confidence, relationships, building empathy, strengthening your community, embracing the differences of others, broadening your lens, reframing negative thoughts and attitudes, etc., I believe the core elements of the change process apply to making any lasting change. The hardest part is taking the first step.

It's no secret that change is hard. Human psychology is quite universal, and at times simple. Unless we are forced to, human nature would rather do less than do more, even if our familiar habits and mindsets are not good in the long term.

No one can force another person to make real change; that must come from within. All it takes is for one moment—one spark—to ignite the will from within to desire change. To create an analogy, the spark is what starts your car. While you may start the car, if you don't drive, you'll never move. Getting to your destination depends on you. Some people may go only as far as recognizing that initial spark. Others may make gratifying, lifelong changes that ripple and spread throughout their lives and the lives of others.

Watershed Moments: The Spark

Life is a series of epiphanies—moments that change the way we see the world or ourselves. Something as simple as watching a ceiling fan spin can permanently change the way an infant sees the world. As infants, we slowly begin to understand the world around us, and our perspectives evolve the more we experience. New discoveries eclipse and rewire old perspectives. When people realize there is something they need to change about their lives, that spark marks the beginning of a new chapter.

When my children were growing up, I felt like I was being pulled in a million different directions, trying to juggle my business career and my family life simultaneously. I vividly remember a defining moment that made me reassess the direction of my life.

I was sitting with my five-year-old son, Michael, while he was having an afternoon snack. In those days, while spending time with my children, I would often pretend to listen, but not actually be present in the moment. That day, while Michael was speaking to me, I decided to turn off autopilot and actively listen. The moment I gave him all my attention, he felt it. He paused and looked at me with an expression that was a mixture of surprise and amazement. I will never forget the joy that radiated from him, being fully heard. He looked at me in a new way, as though I were a stranger to him. His expression told me everything: I had not been listening. Although I may have been there physically, I was not there mentally. I was blind and did not see what truly mattered to me as I carried out my early scripts that were hammered into me: to drive and to succeed.

Many people have said the best actors in the world are children because they are not acting. Children do not edit their behaviors or actions; they act from their honest hearts. Until my children helped me to see otherwise, I was marching through life without questioning my actions. I thought to myself: If I wasn't even listening to my children, what else in my life was I ignoring?

After that initial spark with my son, I made a commitment to become a mother who would be attentive and present in my children's lives. I didn't just make a commitment; I *wanted* to make it. At first, the change process was like laying small bricks one at a time. Slowly, I started to make small improvements. Other times, I would regress and forget about picking up another brick. While I may have regressed, I never stopped stacking bricks. In time, without realizing it, I became a mother both my children felt connected to and looked forward to spending time with. To me, that was the greatest accolade I could ever receive. I didn't know it then, but I was building my cathedral.

Collateral Damage of Early Scripts

Rewriting scripts is a lifelong endeavor that demands an incredible amount of work, like building a cathedral. Throughout my change process, I have stumbled and lost my way many times, forgetting the sparks that got me started.

Despite the watershed moment with my five-year old son, my resolve was often short-lived as I lost focus on building my cathedral. While my eyes were now open to the changes I needed to make in my life, wanting change and making change are two very different things. I found myself slipping back into my old habits, and soon I was back to laying bricks, with no cathedral in sight. Sometimes, it takes a near-death experience to jolt us back into clarity and to get us on the right track again. This was certainly true in my case.

In November of 1995, my life was spinning out of control. I was stressed, full of anxiety, bogged down with international travel, and was simultaneously overcommitted to my life at work and at home. I was barely breathing, let alone functioning. One rainy morning at about 8:30 a.m., I was driving to work in rush-hour traffic. The entrance-ramp speed onto the Beltway was posted at twenty-five miles per hour. I must have been going sixty, thinking only about what I needed to do at work that day. As I moved into the entrance lane that connected onto the Beltway, my car suddenly began to hydroplane. I lost all control as my car swung wildly and from side to side. I had no control of the steering wheel and felt no connection to the ground. Heading straight into heavy oncoming traffic, all I could utter was "Oh my God, oh my God. This is the end." I thought of my children, and how grateful I was that they were not there with me, experiencing this terror.

Right before my car was about to skid onto the Beltway, I smashed into a lamppost. The impact spun my car around like a top—luckily on to the side of the road. In a surreal moment, the lamppost fell backward into the entrance lane, away from the path of oncoming traffic, which would have been disastrous. As I sat in a daze, all I could feel was a sense of amazement that I was still alive and unhurt.

Shortly thereafter, an ambulance arrived and I was asked if I needed a ride to the hospital. I checked myself, and to everyone's amazement, I was fine. My car, on the other hand, had extensive damage. Eventually, a tow truck came to transport my car to a garage. I arrived at the shop, finished the paperwork, rented a car, drove to my office, and worked the entire day, as though nothing had happened.

In reflection, I would like to believe I got through the day because of the shock I had just experienced. Instead, what I remember most was feeling proud of myself for not missing work that day. Looking back, what was scarier than nearly getting killed that morning was how disconnected I had become. Here I was, lucky to be alive, and what I was most happy about was only missing a couple hours out of the workday. I was still brainwashed by my old scripts: don't be a wimp, push forward at any cost.

Even to this day, I shudder at the thought of what could have happened. Had my car skidded a couple of feet to the right or left, who knows how many people I may have killed, along with myself, that morning? I think about what would have happened if that lamppost fell in the other direction, onto oncoming Beltway traffic. Who knows what damage it could have caused to those innocent drivers? It was a miracle that I survived the accident without a scratch. I can't imagine any other explanation than a divine intervention. While I am not a religious person, I am spiritual. I believe in God or a Spirit or a Higher Power, or whatever you want to call it.

That morning's incident was certainly a wake-up call for me—a second spark. Even though I went through the rest of that day without changing my habits, a seed had been planted, and the more I thought about it, the more I started to wake up. It took many years for me to understand what it meant to truly wake up. While it didn't happen overnight, I was taking baby steps.

In the weeks following the accident, I decided to leave my job and stay at home with my children. I knew I had to reconnect with myself and learn to be present for what mattered most in my life. Walking away from a job that challenged and stimulated me was a terrifying and difficult decision. I felt leaving my job would mark the end of my career and that I would end up being nothing more than a disappointment in the eyes of my family and myself. This irrational fear was drilled into me early on by my upbringing, my parents, and my culture. The thought of not being able to meet my expectations sent deep pangs of shame through my stomach. Our early scripts affect us all, yet we tend to be drawn to certain scripts more than others. Being labeled as a success was one of the strongest scripts I clung to.

I don't believe my parents wanted me to succeed at all costs, including disconnection from my loved ones. Rather, it was my interpretation of the script that drove my actions. In hindsight, I can see that I wasn't even aware that I was carrying out my early scripts. It was as though I was existing on autopilot, without questioning my behavior, self-righteous in my conviction that the way I was living my life was the "right" way.

Meeting Our Unadorned Self

Seeing ourselves honestly and acknowledging our virtues and vices are not easy things to do. We work so hard to accumulate adornments that become our protective shields, metaphorical coats of protection we wear in our professional, personal, and social lives. Adornments come in various physical and emotional forms—stature, wealth, physical fitness, image, moral superiority, and ego.

We are like knights in shining armor, carrying a heavy weight on our shoulders, shielding our true selves from others and even from ourselves. When we meet new people, we often don't introduce our true selves, but rather presentations of our shields, and vice versa. The many people we meet are often hiding in their armor, afraid to show their true selves. When you meet someone who isn't carrying their shield, who is at complete ease with who they are, it's a rare and beautiful moment.

Over the years, I worked hard to create the image of a tough and competent career woman—my shield. I lived with a fallacy that I was strong enough to power through my emotions. I never allowed myself to show weakness, even though I was dying inside. It got to the point where even at home with my children and husband, I couldn't remove my shield; it had become a part of me. In the meantime, my shield was getting heavier, and I was creating a greater distance from my inner self, my family, and all those around me. Until I could truly face my naked self, I was unable to embody the change I desired. There was something incredibly painful and humbling about realizing that who I had become was no longer who I wanted to be. No therapists, coaches, or programs could help me to take the first step to face my naked self—only I could.

We must not confuse building up our inner-self and building another adornment. No amount of adornments can veil who we are on the inside. Against our will, our *true* self shows up in action, especially when under heavy pressure. Our biases, greed, righteousness, defensiveness, and closed-mindedness all pierce through our facade. In my experience, I notice that people carry their heaviest shields at work, where getting ahead matters most, often to their own detriment. There are no two versions of us, regardless of how we wish to be seen. Only you can choose to reflect on the cost of keeping up with the heavy lifting of accumulating exterior adornments.

Lisa, a former coaching client of mine, had a similar experience as Terry, in that she received unexpected feedback from her company that she needed to change her attitude. Her colleagues felt that she was combative, defensive, and unable to take criticism. Although Lisa was an excellent and competent executive, many of her peers did not enjoy working with her and thought she was brushing them off. Most of all, she wasn't able to create genuine human connections.

When I spoke to Lisa about her issues, unsurprisingly, she became highly defensive. Nonetheless, Lisa understood what was at stake, bit her tongue, and agreed to work on her behaviors. Motivated by the idea of a promotion and not by making changes to her character, Lisa approached these criticisms intellectually. For a while, Lisa made surface-level changes, overembellishing her personal image through phony affectations. She started going out to lunch with others in the company, something she never did before. She attempted to chit-chat and make friendly conversation, an unusual gesture for her. She wore a fixed smile, even during our coaching sessions. Although these changes may sound like improvements, they were transparent and disingenuous. She was attempting to make real changes in her personality, but her working relationships continued to suffer. Lisa was putting on an act, and everyone could sense it. Rather than acknowledging her weaknesses head-on, she never moved away from her conditioned tendencies.

Sadly, Lisa wasn't willing to explore what was behind her heavily adorned shield. Lisa's desire to change did not come from the heart, it stemmed from a transactional motive. Her resistance to face her true self was what kept her from making advancements at work and more importantly, her personal connections. Unfortunately, Lisa didn't see the connection between the two. Keeping up with building adornments can be exhausting, and the efforts only further distance one from one's authentic self and from others. Lisa understood the language of change, but did not undertake the work. She talked the talk, but could not walk the walk.

Arrogant Intellect, Coward Heart

We live in a dichotomy between reason and emotion. We like to believe we are all guided by logic and rationality, but we are emotional beings. Intellectual knowledge or awareness doesn't automatically translate into self-acknowledgment or embodied behaviors. Often our knowledge stays in our head as something good to know or nice to do, rather than tangible changes or improvements in lifestyle or habits. Unless we take our learning to heart with vigorous discipline and practice, it will not stick.

I have known many incredibly smart people, as you may too, who can cite a long list of their personal blemishes yet do not take this knowledge and do anything about it. It's the arrogance of our intellect that keeps us from taking action, while the cowardice of our heart lets our intellect run the show.

Fred, a former client of mine and a senior partner at a prestigious law firm, often used to tell me, "Soo, I understand everything you are saying and what I need to do, but don't you have a good article or a book I can read instead? I think reading will help to make things a lot clearer for me." Fred's main coaching goal was to work on his defensive attitude. Fred articulated it well: "Yes, I know, people tell me I get defensive and create unnecessary friction. They probably have a good point. I don't like to hear that. I am ready to do the work to change the situation."

The setback with Fred was that he always had reasons for why he became defensive, and he blamed others for his behavior. Fred couldn't take ownership of his behaviors and actions. Numerous times, I shared my observations with Fred that he needed to move out of his head and explore his defensive trait from his heart, to no avail. I suggested that Fred stay with and explore his feelings and not to run away from them—easier said than done.

Intellectualizing the fact that you have a problem is one thing; acknowledging it is another. It's very painful to look inside and face what you don't like about yourself. Fred's persistence to rely on his intellect was a coping mechanism that stalled his progress. While he was a brilliant and successful lawyer, Fred couldn't muster the courage to acknowledge his shortcomings. It takes a courageous heart to pierce through the veil that our arrogant intellect erects, stubbornly keeping our scripts alive through reasoning and justification. Fred's script conditioned him to avoid emotional introspection—staying tough by avoiding heavy feelings. Sadly, Fred couldn't rewrite his scripts because he couldn't allow himself to become vulnerable.

While individual details may vary, the challenges that come with making change are universally shared among all people, transcending gender, race, or culture. One of the most difficult challenges that my coaching clients experienced was to face their feelings head-on. While they were aware of the mindsets and attitudes that were creating breakdowns, and stated that they were committed to doing the work, many had difficulties facing the truth deep from within. Regardless of age, experience, or social status, it's amazing how little we know when it comes to dealing with our emotions. Many believe their feelings are the obstacles that are in the way of what they want to accomplish. Sadly, I have bought into this hypothesis and became the owner of a cowardly heart that kept me from living a fuller life.

It takes a brave heart to embrace one's feelings. Self-control is often equated with suppressing emotions. We are too proud to admit that we feel hurt by a loved one, nervous during a meeting, or embarrassed about a slip-up. However, shutting down or not embracing emotions will only backfire in the long run. If we don't deal with our feelings, emotions will churn and grow bigger and eventually explode, hurting ourselves and others.

The Chinese character THINK (思) reflects upon our nature. This one character combines two characters: The top part represents the brain; the bottom half represents the heart. The heart is the anchor that carries the brain. The Chinese knew that thinking required a marriage between the brain and the heart. Even though the character was created thousands of years ago, this ancient wisdom is just as true today.

Wouldn't it be delightful to move away from an arrogant intellect to a humble one, and from a cowardly heart to a brave one?

And now here is my secret, a very simple secret:
It is only with the heart that one can see rightly;
what is essential is invisible to the eye.

—*The Little Prince*,
ANTOINE DE SAINT-EXUPÉRY

A Humble Student

Every encounter can be an opportunity for new learning and experience. I have gained some of the most poignant and humbling lessons from some of the least expected places. It's impossible to know from where or from whom we may find these venues for growth, but if you have an open mind and heart, beauty and the possibilities for growth surround us all the time. To grow and to change, we need to be open to all the help and learning we can get.

Two of my wisest teachers were not professors, public figures, or authorities; they were nannies that took care of my two children. I was extremely fortunate to learn from them the connecting power of patience and generosity of heart.

After my first child was born, I was desperate to find a loving caretaker who I could trust my daughter with while I worked and traveled. After several disappointing interviews, I had become terrified at the idea of leaving Sophia alone in the hands of a stranger. One day, I received a call from a lovely woman named Mercedes. Because of the conversational Spanish I attained while living in Mexico, I was able to communicate with her. Even without meeting her in person, I was able to sense her energy over the phone, and felt instant ease. I hung up the phone, looked at my husband and said, "Steve, I found our nanny."

Mercedes came from Nicaragua with little money and minimal education. Despite her modest upbringing, rarely have I experienced so many wonderful human qualities embodied by one person. Placing my baby's well-being into the hands of a stranger was frightening. Several well-meaning friends and acquaintances cautioned me with horror stories about caretakers who would neglect the children they looked after or kidnap the children from their families. We were living in Washington, DC, and had no family or relatives to rely on if something happened. Nonetheless, my intuition told me to put my full heart and trust into Mercedes. My intuition paid off, and she never once broke my trust, always kept her word, and loved our children.

Mercedes went above and beyond her responsibilities. She put her full heart and soul into her job and became part of our family. We loved her just as she loved us. I was always touched by Mercedes's generosity in the way she gave back to us. She would always accommodate our schedules and stay late when necessary. Even though she didn't have much, on birthdays and holidays she bought gifts for the children. I felt at ease during my business travels, knowing Mercedes was looking after my two children. Sadly, Mercedes became ill after a few years of working for us. When she could no longer take care of my children, she recommended her friend Pilar, who, like Mercedes, was a godsend. To this day, my children consider them both second mothers.

One day, I came home from work tired and frustrated. My five-month-old infant son, Michael, was crying hysterically and wouldn't stop. I was quite alarmed, as he rarely cried. After about fifteen minutes, my patience wore thin, and I started to become agitated. Mercedes took Michael from me and rocked him gently in her arms for the next thirty minutes. She held him with kindness, love, and patience radiating from her body. I thought I was watching a saint.

Mercedes gave Michael a kind of love I never received as a child. She taught me that without patience, I couldn't be loving. Ever since, this moment has been etched into my heart. This spark made me realize that I still had a long way to go toward building patience.

Mercedes and Pilar showed my family that human beauty has nothing to do with wealth, social status, or education. Ironically, I have frequently experienced that the more people have, the more narrow-minded and greedy they become. I am forever grateful and indebted to Mercedes and Pilar for their love and devotion to my children. I am most grateful to both of them for helping me see the expansiveness of being a humble student of life.

How can we become a humble student living in pervasive diversity? The most important step is being curious about our conditioned attitudes and increasing our self-awareness. As long as I've been in America, I've resisted adopting the subliminal and ubiquitous culture of race labeling. I resent being defined by my race. It makes me feel alienated and as though I do not belong, a feeling I wouldn't want anyone to feel. Think about when you first meet a neighbor who moves in next door: Do you first see a black, white, Asian, or Hispanic person? Or do you see a kind, quiet, or friendly person, who happens to be black, white, Asian, or Hispanic? This question can be a great way to begin to understand our own lens, mindset, and biases.

As an exercise that anyone can practice anywhere, I pick a random person and jot down or take a mental note of my thoughts and feelings about that person. What was my first impression? Was it their skin color, physical attributes, or gender? Or was it their energy, demeanor, and attitude that radiated from within? This exercise helps me to be aware of where my lens is—whether I was describing a label, a race, a bias, or a person. By training our lens and acknowledging how we assess people, we can shift our lens to see beyond labels and start to see human beings. The more we challenge ourselves to rethink how we see people, the more likely we will nurture a connecting space where we feel welcomed and accepted. Openness is infectious and is a powerful teacher to help us to stay as humble students.

Perseverance

First, we experience a spark. Next, we foster the desire and commitment to make change. Then, we garner the courage to face our unadorned selves. Now, we are in a position to make real strides, but we are only just beginning. The reality is that without perseverance, we cannot make sustainable change. If we are going to set goals and attempt real change, we have to put in time and effort.

Of the many changes that I have worked on in my life, the most important to me was becoming a connecting mother who can influence my children to broaden their lenses. I've felt success and I've felt failure. I've felt proud and I've felt inadequate. The one constant throughout my journey was my perseverance to stay on the path toward making changes that enabled open and connecting dialogues, no matter how discouraged I felt at times.

Awareness of our faults is one thing; ownership is another. It takes a lot of emotional strength to look at ourselves honestly and admit the limitations of our scripts. It can be very discouraging to grasp and admit our shortcomings. Take Fred, for example. He was aware that he had relational issues at work, but the act of self-acknowledgment of this fact was too painful. This mental block is a universal human quality that I've seen hamper many people, including myself.

When we feel shame about our shortcomings, we can either move forward or run back to our comfort zone of old narratives and habits. Our growth process necessitates that we do not feel shame but instead find encouragement from accepting our imperfections. It is moving from "How terrible I am. That's really bad. Shame on me" to that of compassion: "Isn't that interesting? I would like to learn more about it. What can I do differently?"

We live in a fix-it-now culture. We expect instant gratification and miracle solutions without persistence and hard work. While it's tempting to buy into the false promises that crash diets and magic pills sell to us (imagine all those unwanted pounds just melting away!), we know it's unrealistic to think that a quick fix can lead to permanent changes. There is no such thing as a silver bullet that will deliver lifelong results—other than our own work.

Nothing can better predict results than one's mental framework: fast and impatient may lead to short-term results but long-term frustrations; slow and sustained may take longer but can lead to lasting success. For one hour, try switching everything you do with your dominant hand with the other. I imagine it would be pretty difficult. Yet through perseverance, that scratchy handwriting will become more legible, and in time, you'll feel comfortable using your less dominant hand. The same can be said about our efforts to alter old beliefs and habits, removing ourselves from our deeply imprinted scripts, biases, or behaviors.

Self-Empowerment

Changing the way we feel about ourselves can empower us, help us accept others' differences, and nourish human connection. To my heartwarming surprise, an eighth-grade student struggling with her racial identity reached out to me for advice after finding me on the Internet. While she hasn't experienced discrimination, she is anxious that she will eventually become a victim of racism. How could she not be anxious? We live in a climate that has conditioned us to become hypervigilant about racism. I believe that she, like many others, is at a crossroads: Will she allow the influence of others to define her worldview and sense of self or will she take ownership of her own identity?

Attaining a secure sense of self is a universal challenge that transcends race, gender, background, sexual orientation, age, or culture. It's almost impossible to remove ourselves from external stimuli, especially in this social climate where people are being defined and judged on narrow physical dimensions such as race, gender, ethnicity, and online presence.

Through my journey of becoming comfortable in my own skin, I learned that I am the only person who can help me. The process I've been practicing to bring out my expanded self has been to embrace, acknowledge, and own my damaging downward spirals without making excuses or placing blame. It takes courage to admit one's self-defeating patterns. It is not an easy thing to pull yourself up when you are down; however, we can't give up if we want to change.

How do we attain an empowered self? To begin, we must embrace our own insecurities. Being insecure is being human. Think about the negative effects of self-defeating expressions, such as: "I'm stupid," "I suck," "I'm different," "I'm awkward," "I'm not equal," "I am afraid," "I'm misunderstood," "I don't belong," "People don't like me," and so on. These kinds of thoughts keep us small, contracted, and defensive.

Once we become aware of the voice in our head and acknowledge the narrative we tell ourselves, only then can we change our story by reframing the narrative. This effort requires constant commitment to tug ourselves upward, until our new beliefs and narratives about who we are become a part of our embodied core. Amazingly, something as simple as changing the negative voice in your head to say, "I am a unique individual and I feel good to be who I am!" can shift your entire being. Your mood, your voice, and your expression all will change. Positive self-talk can be so liberating and expansive. Try this right now. Pick something that you usually beat yourself up over and flip the script. Now, imagine how you would feel if you could keep that voice with you every day, because you can.

Your sense of self is defined by the voice in your head. That voice is the author of your mindset, behavior, and actions. It can be positive or negative, loving or fearful, empowered or victimized. You get to choose which story you want to embody and believe in: your own or someone else's.

Humans are assumption-making machines. Our perceptions of others are actually projections of ourselves. The moment we make an assumption about someone else is the moment we eliminate the possibilities of learning about that person. This is the foundation of our diversity challenge. Assumptions and blaming hinder our own growth and connection. Living from a place of not knowing as a humble student provides us with a space to question and clarify our inner voices. This is true empowerment.

Expand Your Possibilities

None of us had a choice where we were born. We didn't get to choose what type of script we'd be imprinted with, the parents who would raise us, or the culture we adopted. As an adult, we have the opportunity to expand our possibilities beyond what we thought were our boundaries. We have a choice to examine the old scripts that we carry. By taking a chance and discovering the changes we want to make in our lives, we can begin the process of rewriting scripts and changing our mindsets and behaviors. We alone have the ability to change the way we think, feel, perceive, and connect with others. By rewriting scripts, we shift our deep-rooted lenses, alter our biases, and connect through human commonalities.

Human connection beyond labels, political correctness, and limiting scripts is the catapulting fuel for building an authentic and pervasive diversity. Our capacity to connect with others affects everything we do and every relationship we build. Connections are felt by the energy we emit, not so much the words we use. Words that people say can be manufactured; intrinsic energy cannot.

The beauty of change is that we harvest the rippling and synergistic effects of growth that continue to enrich our lives and relationships. As our mindset shifts, so does our behavior; as our behavior shifts, so does our mindset. As we open up our hearts to broaden, we increase our inner joy and happiness. As we share and radiate our energy, we touch those around us, who can then inspire others to open themselves up and connect.

When I described this book to my friend Chuck, I told him how I would be exploring the racial tensions that are blocking pervasive diversity and our ability to connect despite differences. Chuck smiled and said, "That's great, Soo. Your subject is very timely. So what's the solution?"

As I mentioned before, everyone wants a fix-it-now solution. Changes rarely happen quickly or smoothly. Changing diversity culture and bridging the racial divide are no different. When we are dealing with human emotions, racial divides, diversity challenges, and shifting individual mindsets, it's unrealistic to assume we can solve all our problems with a formula, an ideology, or written rules. The conflicts we wrestle with today in regard to diversity and the racial divide by no means stem from a lack of analysis, strategy, or enforcement. Humans are not machines; we cannot just hit the reset button and hope everything falls into the right place.

The world is rich because we are different. The world is challenged because we are different. With increased awareness and empathy, our eyes can see beyond visible differences and our hearts can embrace universally shared human essences. Building new imprints is a lifelong journey for an individual and for a nation. Change and growth is a revolving cycle with no end. The diversity journey we started years ago may not even be close to its final destination. To move forward, we may have to step back and take a moment to reflect and reassess.

We are living in new times and therefore need new measures. Our mindsets are evolving, and we need alternatives that align with our shifting world. No rules or measures will satisfy everyone or fix all our racial and diversity issues. Nevertheless, we cannot prolong the racial tensions and hostilities that have hampered diversity advancements. We may never find a perfect tomorrow, but we can have a better one.

What divides us and what connects us? The answer can only lie within us. Biases, prejudices, greed, and self-righteousness divide us. Awareness, broadening, empathy, and openness connect us. Regardless of who we are in our diverse world, each of us possesses the ability, the power, and the responsibility to change and grow. We are the captains of our own vessels who can redirect and reorient our course. We must do our part in striving toward unity and harmony. As we change and broaden, society as a whole will shift with us. As society changes, diversity culture will change with it. Along the way, without realizing it, together we can change from being foreigners within to building beautiful cathedrals.

Essential Takeaways

- Imagine living with a secure sense of self that empowers you to be who you are in your personal and professional life. What would emerge and shift within you? What voices in your head might be in the way of moving forward? What will it take for you to initiate your empowered self?
- Through personal growth and self-empowerment, collectively we advance pervasive diversity. By changing and broadening, we open our eyes from within, pay attention to what we see, gain empathy to see through others' eyes, and create space that embraces who we and others are.

ACKNOWLEDGMENTS

This is a book about human connection that transcends our outer and inner differences. I am indebted to my countless encounters across races, cultures, beliefs, and languages. They have taught me that through our shared humanity we can build harmonious diversity where we can connect and flourish together.

I am most grateful to my loving family: my husband and life-long companion, Steve; my devoted son, Michael; my fearless daughter, Sophia, and her caring husband, Rob, for their unwavering love, encouragement, support, and time while writing this book.

I am honored and grateful for Clarence Page's most thoughtful and heartfelt foreword. As a Pulitzer Prize–winning syndicated columnist and senior member of the *Chicago Tribune* editorial board, Clarence has been devoted to race and identity issues, a position that has been inspirational and influential.

Special thanks to my agent, Jeff Herman, for believing in my message, and Michael Pye, associate publisher at Red Wheel/Weiser for seeing the value of my content and bringing it to life. My sincere gratitude to my supportive team at Red Wheel/Weiser: Jane Hagaman, Christine LeBlond, Kathryn Sky-Peck, Laurie Kelly, Bonni Hamilton, Eryn Carter Eaton, Mike Conlon, and Michelle Spanedda for your support in editing, cover design, production, and marketing.

For help in completing my project, I owe much appreciation to Mark Malatesta, Amy Osmond Cook, and Brad Wright. I am grateful to my friends Hedy Schleifer, Marie Balian, Kitana Kattan, Rita Silverman, Gary Weinstein, and Rich and Gaye Christiansen who went out of their way to give me their time, affirmation, and advice.

NOTES

Chapter 1

1. Jeffrey M. Jones, "Record-High 77% of Americans Perceive Nation as Divided," Gallup, Politics, Nov 21, 2016, *http://news.gallup.com.* Accessed August 3, 2020.

2. Michael Smith and Lydia Saad, "Economy Top Problem in a Crowded Field," Gallup, Economy, December 19, 2016, *http://news.gallup.com.* Accessed August 3, 2020.

3. Art Swift, "Americans' Worries About Race Relations at Record High," Gallup Politics, March 15 2017, *http://news.gallup.com.* Accessed August 3, 2020.

4. Anna Brown, "Key Findings on Americans' Views of Race in 2019," Pew Research Center, April 9, 2019, *www.pewresearch.org.* Accessed August 3, 2020.

5. John Whitesides, "From Disputes to a Breakup: Wounds Still Raw after U.S. Election," *Reuters*, Special Reports, February 7, 2017, *www.reuters.com.* Accessed August 3, 2020.

6. Frank Newport, "In U.S., 87% Approve of Black-White Marriage, vs. 4% in 1958: Ninety-six Percent of Blacks, 84% of Whites Approve," Gallup, Politics, July 25, 2013, *http://news.gallup.com.* Accessed August 3, 2020.

Chapter 3

1. OECD Data, Mathematics Performance (PISA); Science Performance (PISA), *https://data.oecd.org*. Accessed August 4, 2020.

2. Ana Singh, The "Scourge of South Korea": Stress and Suicide in Korean Society, *Berkeley Political Review*, October 31, 2017, *https://bpr.berkeley.edu*. Accessed August 4, 2020.

3. Kenneth Burke quotes, *www.inspiringquotes.us/*. Accessed August 1, 2020.

Chapter 6

1. John A. Lucy, "Sapir-Whorf Hypothesis," *ScienceDirect*, *www.sciencedirect.com*. Accessed August 4, 2020.

2. Betty Birner, "Does the Language I Speak Influence the Way I Think?" Linguistic Society of America, *www.linguisticsociety.org*. Accessed August 4, 2020.

Chapter 8

1. Jennifer L. Eberhardt, Nilanjana Dasgupta, and Tracy L. Banaszynski, "Believing Is Seeing: The Effects of Racial Labels and Implicit Beliefs on Face Perception," National Library of Medicine, *https://pubmed.ncbi.nlm.nih.gov*. Accessed August 4, 2020.

2. Frank Dobbin and Alexandra Kalev, "Why Diversity Programs Fail," *Harvard Business Review*, July–August 2016 Issue, *https://hbr.org*. Accessed August 4, 2020.

3. "Health, United States, 2015: With Special Feature on Racial and Ethnic Health Disparities, Table 1 Resident Population by Age, Sex, Race, and Hispanic Origin: United States, Selected Years 1950–2014," NCBI (National Center for Biotechnology Information), *www.ncbi.nlm.nih.gov*. Accessed October 6, 2020.

4. "Percent Minority: 1970–2042," United States Census Bureau, *https://www.census.gov.* Accessed October 11, 2020.

Chapter 9

1. "Race and Ethnicity in the United States Census," Wikipedia, *https://en.wikipedia.org.* Accessed August 5, 2020.

2. Sandra L. Colby and Jennifer M. Ortman, "Projections of the Size and Composition of the U.S. Population: 2014 to 2060," Table 2, United States Census Bureau, March 2015, *www.census.gov.* Accessed August 5, 2020.

3. Karen R. Humes, Nicholas A. Jones, and Roberto R. Ramirez, "Overview of Race and Hispanic Origin: 2010," United States Census Bureau, March 1, 2011, *www.census.gov.* Accesssed October 6, 2020.

4. Jens Manuel Krogstad and D'vera Cohn, "U.S. Census Looking at Big Changes in How It Asks about Race and Ethnicity," Pew Research Center, March 14, 2014, *www.pewresearch.org.* Accessed October 6, 2020.

Chapter 10

1. "Congress and the Public: Congress and the Public," Gallup, *http://news.gallup.com.* Accessed August 21, 2020.

2. "Stanford Prison Experiment, August 15–21, 1971," Stanford Libraries, *https://exhibits.stanford.edu.* Accessed August 5, 2020.

INDEX

ABOUT THE AUTHOR

As a strategy consultant and executive coach to multinational corporations, Soo Bong Peer comes from a multicultural upbringing with over thirty years of experience in strategic marketing, global branding, business development, international joint ventures, and leadership development. Soo is also a writer with a keen interest in diversity and race relations.

Raised in a South Korean military, political, and diplomatic family, Soo grew up in South Korea, Mexico, the UK, Japan, and the United States. Soo is a naturalized American citizen and lives in the United States. Having journeyed wide polarities in cultures, people, social statuses, political regimes, and businesses, Soo believes that human connection is the foundation for building a world of pervasive diversity.

Throughout her hands-on business career managing and working with a wide range of colleagues from diverse backgrounds, including, race, gender, culture, nationality, and disciplines, Soo acutely experienced many conflicts arising from diversity issues that generated unease, distrust, and resentment. Soo learned that across functional areas within a company, the underlying emotions employees felt toward diversity drove employee engagement, retention, and competitiveness. Soo is well aware that constructing diversity programs that employees embrace goes far beyond diversity statistics or training. She believes that we must find a sustainable path to bridge diversity goals, human psychology, and bottom-line pressure.

Companies Soo has been affiliated with as an employee, strategy consultant, or executive coach include Bell Canada; Booz, Allen & Hamilton; CNN/Turner; Comsat; ExxonMobil; Global One (Deutsche Telekom, France Telecom, Sprint Alliance); IBM; Inter-American Development Bank; Leo Burnett Worldwide; Mars; MetLife HealthCare; and Ogilvy & Mather.

Soo earned an MBA from Darden School of Business, University of Virginia; a master's degree in biochemistry from Boston University Medical Center; and a bachelor's degree in chemistry from College of Notre Dame of Maryland. In addition, she has a Leadership Coaching Certification from Georgetown University and is International Coach Federation certified.

Married for thirty-six years with two biracial children, Soo and her husband live in Park City, Utah.